It Isn't Always
BLACK
OR
WHITE

Reflections of a High School Principal

During Nashville's Integration

J. Mack Hargis

J. MACK HARGIS, PhD

Fulton Books, Inc.
Meadville, PA

Published by Fulton Books 2020

ISBN 978-1-64654-487-5 (paperback)
ISBN 978-1-64654-488-2 (digital)

Printed in the United States of America

CONTENTS

FOREWORD

Let me say, first off, that Dr. Hargis was a very popular teacher, coach, and school administrator. His faculty, students, and community adored him. He is personable, intelligent, inquisitive, empathetic—a natural problem solver. Mack was never haughty or braggadocious, and you would never have known he held a PhD from Peabody/Vanderbilt University unless someone, other than himself, told you.

I met Mack in 1983. I was teaching middle school, and he was principal of DuPont High School. We were adjunct professors teaching leadership for a local university at their off-site campuses. We often traveled together to classes in Memphis, Chattanooga, and other locations around the state. We spent a lot of time together, sharing our weekly stories. We are both storytellers at heart, so there was rarely a lapse in conversation. We became instant friends and remain so to this day. As you read the book, you will find yourself wanting to cry, laugh—and at times—feel as if you're riding in the car with us on weekly university-seminar trips.

This book is not an academic pursuit for a leading educational journal, but an attempt to share with you what life was like as an educator during these pioneer times. These stories will inspire you. We were breaking new ground for sure. Teachers were tough; they had to be dedicated, caring, and professional. I deeply admire this first wave of pioneers. They made it a lot easier for those of us who followed.

What educators faced was primarily a black-white-integration issue that was nonnegotiable as so ordered by the federal court. In many ways, educators were the guinea pigs, as were the students. As an educator, it wasn't uncommon to be labeled a racist by both sides on the same day. It was a time of stress, exhaustion, intense emotions, and sometimes, physical volatility.

It was a time that called for great servant leadership. It was a time for someone with great common sense—coupled with superior intellect and competence—a time for a visionary, and someone who inspires and motivates—a serious leader. But a leader with a sense of humor as well—a time for a leader who was just as comfortable hanging out with custodians, cafeteria workers, and bus drivers as he was rubbing shoulders with city leaders. The times called for a restart, a rebirth. Thus, step forward the renaissance men and women.

Mack was such a leader.

—Paul Doyle, EdD
Author, School Superintendent, and College Professor

PREFACE

I parked my truck in front of the Nashville Board of Education Administration building and hesitated before going inside. *Am I doing the right thing?* kept pouring through my mind like a swollen creek flooding over the banks, pushing everything out of its way. It was a stifling hot July day, and as the truck door opened, heat rushed in around me as if I had stepped into a raging sauna. Sweat began to pop out on my brow while cold chills dashed up and down my spine. I slowly moved toward the building entrance and managed to push myself through the front door and stood there for a few seconds, embracing the cool air.

Seeing the door marked "Insurance and Retirement" caused my stomach to tighten and become slightly nauseated. I had an appointment to discuss my retirement. I was forty-five years old, had two teenage girls, and a wife who was a teacher. My mind hammered with, *Is this the right thing?*

I entered the retirement office and sat down with the lady in charge. After one hour of discussion, it was determined that my retirement funds would be enough for my family to survive, but I would have to hustle to make enough money for the girls to go to college. Leaving the office, my mind was still spinning. I began thinking about the past and things that had transpired in my twenty-five years with the Nashville Metro Board of Education. In everyone's career, events that alter life's perceived plans occur that they have no control. *If you want to make God laugh, just tell Him how you have your life planned* was the phrase that shot through my mind. I have made Him chuckle several times.

My particular nimbus was the federal court-ordered integration of black and white schools in Nashville, Tennessee. This was not a smooth, well-planned court order. It was handed down abruptly that allowed very little time or concern for planning. As I left the school board and cut through the thick, steamy humidity to my truck, my mind began to relive the events that had prepared me for the forced altering of my life plans.

Being from Milan, a small West Tennessee town, my upbringing was not void of interactions with black individuals. These experiences were definitely a positive influence on my professional demeanor. The term that the news media and other leaders used to describe the situation that consumed the Nashville public school system was "integration."

ACKNOWLEDGMENTS

The original intent of writing this memoir was for my family. However, while taking a writing course from a professor at Vanderbilt University, this premise changed. When he read a few of the stories, he said to me, "These are history, and they should be preserved and published."

Completing this manuscript was a journey, and I owe thanks to many:

- Encouragement to move forward came from my writing group, Carole Rietz, Kathy Bennett, Lyonel Gilmer, and Jerry Henderson. Dr. Henderson was invaluable in structuring this book and became affectionately known as my "Grammar Cop."
- Thanks also to Heather Pelc at Fulton Publishing for her insight, knowledge, and availability throughout the publishing process.
- My sincere appreciation additionally goes to all the dedicated educators that I had the privilege to work alongside throughout my career.
- Finally, thanks go to my wife, Ann, daughters, Heather and Rachel, son-in-law, Stephen Kennedy, and grandchildren, Connor and Lauren, for giving me a reason to share these stories. Heather was invaluable in guiding me through the editing and publication process.

LOOKING BACK

Internal raging temperature and gut-wrenching turmoil of what might have been clashed with a calm understanding of what reality had in store. My lot in life, as well as many others in my profession, was to aid in the correction of yesteryear's selfish and inhuman decisions.

Each individual, as he treads the road laid out for him, carries the benefits and deficits of his environment to which there is generally no input. These early environmental rules and regulations will be wrestled with until we pass through the eternal veil.

The environment chosen for me by the gods was a small West Tennessee town, where attitudes and expectations were homogenous in nature. Any misaligned childhood activities were corrected, not only by family but by any adult that viewed them.

Correction not only took place by the community but, again, when one arrived home. Rules were to be accepted and obeyed by all youth. Any objection to the rules was considered backtalk. Backtalk was the cardinal rule that was never permitted to be broken.

This small town allowed two major activities for the youth: working and sports. If employment eluded you, your family would intervene and help you acquire a job. My first job was not one of my seeking but one that my grandparents graciously procured for me. This job was chopping cotton at the tender age of nine. It consisted of us arriving at the cotton field, weather permitting, at 7:30 a.m. and thinning out the small cotton plant sprouts with a hoe. Thinning the sprouts encouraged stronger and better yielding plants, thus, a higher production of cotton. While carefully thinning the young cotton plants, we also cleaned the row of all foulous, also known as weeds and grass. This hoeing or chopping was done until noon when the much-anticipated lunchtime came. Lunch usually consisted of a sandwich, cold fried chicken, water, and maybe a cookie. After lunch, we went back to the field where the sun had gained momentum and blistered down with all its fury, sparing no one. Everyone worked together in the field: men, women, boys, girls, black, and white. The only exception to the day's work was lunch. The white and black ate in separate groups, one of the environmental rules that was accepted and never questioned.

Later that year, I was delivered back to the same cotton patch to observe what our efforts had accomplished and to harvest the crop. This was better known to all as "picking cotton." The same group that chopped in the spring was there to pick the cotton. When chopping cotton, I could almost hold my own with the others. Picking that white fluffy stuff was a different matter. My best day of picking cotton was a little over one hundred pounds. My fellow laborers or, in this case, older competitors could bring in two to three hundred pounds a day by picking two rows at a time. I could hardly keep up when working one row. I was shamed by their friendly teasing but would not—no, could not—slip away in disgrace due to my grandparents being in the field with me. I also wanted the large remittance of three cents or maybe four cents a pound if other farmers were in competition for cotton pickers. These jobs were hot, backbreaking, poor paying, and seasonal. About three to four dollars a day was my top pay.

My brother had a paper route, which appeared to be a better opportunity. I applied to deliver the *Commercial Appeal,* a Memphis morning paper. This job gave me my first insight into the varied levels of my environment/community. Delivering and collecting money for the newspaper allowed me a peek into many homes. Seeing the diversity in homes and furnishings was a revelation to me. Each area of the community reflected a level of success. Once a person achieved monetary prosperity, he was eligible to navigate up the pecking order. This advancement was done by moving into the upscale part of the community. There was one exception: a successful Negro could not move into a white community no matter his wealth. The black community had their own pecking order similar to that of the whites.

I carried papers to everyone—black, white, residential, commercial—and maintained a good relationship with all my customers. Overall, it was a good job with few hardships. Adjustments were made for these inconveniences, and after a short while, these were considered routine. The two major adjustments were forcing myself out of bed at 4:00 a.m. each day and the slow-pay customers that required me to return numerous times to collect payment. Interestingly enough, most of these individuals resided in the highest-pecking order of the white community.

Having a job that terminated about 6:30 a.m. each day, seven days a week, left plenty of time for another job in the summer according to my father's way of thinking. He, through his connections, got me one of the most envied positions in the entire community: digging ditches for sewer lines and, of course, when necessary, cleaning clogged sewers. This job was completed each day at 5:00 p.m. In essence, I was employed during the summer from 4:00 a.m. to 5:00 p.m., which left little time to violate the community rules.

The ditch-digging job gave me the opportunity to view my community from another perspective. The crew consisted of five black men (Homer, Cletus, John, Tom, and Hosie), along with my best friend, Marc Horton. After initial introduction and developing an understanding of one another, we settled into our assigned task and worked together as a team. In a nutshell, the job consisted of handling concrete sewer pipes four feet long and eight inches in diameter. They were lowered into ditches with depths from three to twelve feet. Once the pipes were at the bottom of the ditch, they were leveled to grade and glued together with hot tar.

Work went on with pleasant bantering back and forth, which made the day pass faster. During lunch, we sometimes ate together, which was different from my cotton-picking experience. At times, we would swap a sandwich for a fried chicken leg while we joked about personal experiences.

My favorite crew member was Hosie. A slender tall man of about forty with a slick thin mustache that gave him a dashing look when he smiled. My attraction to him was his ability to continue with a constant flow of what is commonly called bull. No one ever knew where the truth lay in his comments. Another designating feature was limping on his right leg. One day at lunch, he pulled off his tattered brownish-black work boot. His bootless foot revealed a stump with only a heel and half a foot. My astonishment at this deformed foot and his ability to carry his workload without uttering a complaint caused me to blurt out, "What in the world happened to your foot?"

Hosie, without hesitation, said, "I lost it during the war."

A large bucket of renewed respect was poured over me for this man. That night, my newfound information about Hosie was shared with my father.

My father smiled and said, "Who is the source of this information?"

"Hosie."

My father's smile broadened as he replied, "Hosie was born that way."

Was respect lost for Hosie? No, just a bigger filter was installed to decipher his rattling. At the end of each day, we would go back to our respective corners of the community, only to return the following day to reunite and accomplish the task set before us while joking and thickly spreading BS.

Interestingly enough, those backbreaking jobs that my dad and others in my family acquired for me was a way of planning my future. My understanding of this concept did not come until later in life. Hot, dirty and backbreaking work was a subtle but effective way of encouraging a person to go to college.

The other avenue that the community provided for those who were interested and had God-given body coordination was sports. Baseball, football, and basketball were the items spread on the table for selection. Most talented athletics engaged in all activities. My selection was basketball, which in retrospect was puzzling as my ninth-grade year found me only five feet, four inches tall and weighing a daunting one hundred pounds. My size or lack of it was not an issue as it never occurred to me that I was smaller than my mates. Many times, when an obvious limitation in one's physique is not pointed out, that individual does not see it.

During junior high school, an event took place that brought me in touch with the black segment of the community once again. The gymnasium used by the white community was known as the "barn" due to its openness, large permanent seats, and draftiness that made it impossible to keep warm unless it was filled with body heat from a large crowd. This gymnasium was old and should be replaced, but during this area, you never threw anything away that had usability. The old gym burned to the ground. No one knew or at least didn't tell how the fire started. This presented two dilemmas for the community: how to prepare the present high school basketball teams for the season and a new athletic facility must be funded and built with all haste.

The high school for black students worked out a schedule where both teams could use their gym to practice. The junior high team, which I was aspiring to be part of, held their practice on an outside dirt court just a short distance from the charred basketball barn. We practiced in mud, cold, and snow, but just before the tournament, we were allowed to practice for a few days in the black gymnasium. The gym was not exceptionally large but was well-equipped. I was impressed with the facility and thought that the term "separate but equal" was definitely true in our community.

As time passed, I found myself in high school. I made the basketball team thanks to the seven inches and fifty-five pounds that were added to my frame. Our team won its way to the state tournament that was held in Nashville. The school year was 1959–60 and unrest was taking place in Downtown Nashville. Negroes were demanding the right to eat at the restaurants by staging what was called "sit-ins."

Our team was staying at the Maxwell House Hotel. Coach Milton Mayo gave us the run of the city with orders to be back at a certain time. We took off to explore Nashville, and the first stop was Woolworth. My stomach was controlling my actions, and it demanded to be satisfied. I walked into Woolworth and, after a quick survey, found the food counter. I rushed over to find a seat, which was difficult as most were filled with young black individuals. Finding an open seat between two young black men, I settled in and waved to a waitress. The two young black men looked at me with smirks on their faces. When the waitress arrived, I placed my order for a hamburger and fries. She gave me a look that projected complete and utter disgust.

Without hesitation, she said, "This counter is closed!"

I blurted out, "Why?"

She gave me another disgusted, filthy look that indicated she was talking to a very stupid person.

"Just look at them," she said as she waved her hands.

I replied, "So?"

She coldly looked at me and reaffirmed the counter was closed and walked away.

I sat there for a few minutes, contemplating my next move. My stomach was growling, and the hungry pains would not be denied. As I moved away from the counter, I felt two pats on my back. Still not completely grasping the situation and the historical significance, I made my way to the Krystal for two ten-cent hamburgers and a bowl of their delicious chili.

Basketball continued to dominate my life in college as I was fortunate enough to play for Lambuth University. I moved out of my community with its set of rules and into a similar community and similar rules. My life was uneventful except for visits to Lane University. Lane University was an all-black college located a few miles away. Several members of our team would go to Lane and watch their basketball team. Lane had a player by the name of Willie Martin. He was the best basketball player I had ever seen. We would go to watch him and learn from his moves. We enjoyed our outings to Lane and marveled at Willie's ability. These outings were enjoyed for the years at Lambuth, and then my 1964 graduation disrupted my simple but pleasant life.

Looking for a teaching and coaching job could be a complete book within itself. The Nashville school system offered me a job. Going to a large city was an eye-popping education for this small-town boy.

The Metro Nashville Schools had just begun to integrate due to a federal court order. First, the faculty would be integrated, black teachers into white schools, and white teachers into black schools. Students were allowed to attend the closest school.

My first in-service training was held at Cameron High School, a black school with academic and athletic pride. When lunchtime came, I took a shortcut through the gymnasium to the parking lot. That is when I saw the difference. All the equipment was old and outdated. The facilities and equipment appeared substandard. As I asked questions, I was told that much of the materials at the black schools were actually hand-me-downs from the white schools. This revelation was unsettling for me and challenged my separate but equal community learned law.

My first assignment was an elementary school located close to the governor's mansion. This was a very pleasant and uneventful year. My second assignment was Litton Junior High School with coaching responsibilities. Football, basketball, and track were the sports that were assigned to me. My first love, basketball, gave me personal satisfaction as we won the championship two out of the three years I was at Litton Junior. We also won a Nashville city track championship.

I was promoted to assistant high school basketball coach at Litton High School. At the same time, I was offered a head basketball coach's position at a college in Alabama. I declined the college position due to my recent promotion and there being approximately twenty high schools in Nashville. I felt the opportunity for a head basketball position was just around the corner. I was told that my name was at the top of the list. Also, another factor that influenced my decision was the Alabama college position paid less than the five thousand dollars that I was receiving from the Nashville school system.

My life's goals were moving in the right direction when suddenly, a black cloud of turmoil came out of nowhere in the form of a decision from the federal court. The Nashville schools were moving too slowly integrating the school system. Therefore, a plan approved by the court was mandated, and the school system was legally bound to implement it. This plan changed my life and goals. With the stroke of a pen, the federal court reduced the number of high schools in Metro Nashville from twenty plus to thirteen. Simple math revealed that, suddenly, there were seven unemployed head high school basketball coaches in the Metro Nashville school system. The chances of a person such as myself getting a high school basketball coaching position was slightly below nil.

Soul-searching and goal reevaluation had to be done. There was no time to lament prior decisions as those opportunities were gone in the wind. Integration is a word that reverberates in many dimensions for all who experienced it. They can allow themselves to descend into the muck of despair or raise their eyes and know that they were a part of a one-hundred-year metamorphosis.

First Jobs in Education

Glendale Elementary

TACKLING THE WORLD

Like most graduates, my ambition was to change the world, especially my world of basketball. My primary goal in life was to coach basketball and win as many state championships as possible. With that goal in mind, I started interviewing with school systems in West Tennessee.

I was offered several jobs, but the one that was most unusual and noteworthy was at Whiteville, Tennessee. My duties were to coach boys' and girls' basketball teams, teach health, physical education, and history. I also was to manage the gymnasium area and keep it clean, along with driving a school bus. My salary was to be three thousand two hundred dollars a year, but if I had a winning basketball season, the booster club would give me a bonus of two hundred dollars. After considering this position and other offers, it was obvious I needed advice.

Fortunately, Mr. Thomas, the superintendent of my hometown school system, lived three houses from where I was raised. An appointment was made to discuss my situation. After listening to me, he gave me excellent advice, which was related to early decisions he had made about his career.

He said, "Mack, if I had it to do over, I would probably go to a much-larger school system. A larger school system gives a person more opportunity for advancement."

Mr. Thomas's advice made sense to me, which resulted in accepting a job in Nashville, Tennessee, as an elementary teacher. My salary was three thousand six hundred dollars per year. This was not coaching, but I felt that I could work into a coaching position in a few years. Also, I would be making two hundred dollars more a year than the other offers. Interestingly, the Metro Nashville school system gave the teachers a raise that year that had not been included in the original salary. My starting salary was suddenly four thousand, two hundred dollars a year. Not bad, a six-hundred-dollar raise, and I had not started to work.

BIG PICTURE
AT
MARTHA VAUGHT

Martha Vaught Elementary

Scheduling Dilemma

My first assignment was teaching physical education at two elementary schools, Martha Vaught and Glendale, located approximately seven miles apart. The principals gave me my schedule at the beginning of the year, which allowed for thirty minutes travel between schools. The second semester, it was my responsibility to arrange my time.

After talking with the Martha Vaught teachers about their preferences, I arranged my day with ninety minutes travel time. This allowed for a nice lunch without cafeteria noise, and I could have a choice of food. It worked well for the first three weeks.

My supervisor, Mr. Harris, had reviewed the schedules of all elementary school physical education teachers. After discovering my unique schedule, he paid me a visit.

I was asked to report to the principal's office at Martha Vaught. When I entered, Mr. Harris was sitting behind the principal's desk.

He motioned for me to sit and said, "Mr. Hargis, can you give me justification for the large amount of time you have allocated for travel?"

I knew I was in trouble. My mind raced, trying to find an acceptable explanation.

"Mr. Harris, sometimes the traffic is congested, and I wanted to make sure I arrived promptly."

Mr. Harris gave me a questioning look and said, "I managed to travel the few miles in much less time."

"I thought I would stop and have lunch on the way," I sheepishly replied.

Mr. Harris leaned back in his chair, and with a half grin on his face, he said, "I think all traveling physical education teachers would like this schedule, but it is not going to work. Rearrange the schedule and have it on my desk tomorrow and eliminate your lunch hour on the road."

I complied with his mandate, and my revised schedule was on his desk the next day with the original thirty minutes travel time. He was right, I was wrong, but nothing ventured, nothing gained, and I wasn't fired.

I had to give my new schedule to the principals. They were different as daylight and dark. Martha Vaught's principal was fun-loving and a very efficient manager. I went into her office and gave her my new schedule.

She looked at it, smiled, and said, "They wouldn't let you get away with it, huh? If other physical education teachers found out about your schedule, they would complain, therefore causing problems. Supervisors don't like problems."

Young Black Men

Martha Vaught School was my morning position; after lunch, I would drive to Glendale. I was in my office at Martha Vaught, which was the boiler room. They supplied me an old desk that had been pushed in a corner under several pressure gauges. I had just straightened up my desk and was going out the door when Mrs. Adams came bursting through the door. She was excited, breathing hard, and yelled, "Wait a minute! Wait a minute! I want to talk with you."

I thought to myself, *What have I done now?* "Yes, ma'am, what do you need?"

She grabbed my arm and pulled me back into the boiler room and said in an excitedly hushed tone, "There are some black boys playing basketball on the court."

"Is that a problem?"

"Yes, they are disturbing Mrs. Rogers's class."

"Okay, do you want them to leave?" I asked.

There were four young black men playing basketball on the asphalt court. I still remember the ball they were using. It was an old worn leather ball that had begun to peel. When they shot at the goal, it looked like a wounded bird flopping through the air.

I watched them for a few minutes, admiring their abilities. What I really wanted to do was pull my shirt off and join them, but what you want to do and what you have to do is generally not the same thing. They had just completed one game and were ready to start another. I took the opportunity during the pause to get their attention. They stopped playing and acknowledged my coming on the court. Three of the young men were a head taller than me, and the fourth was about my height and built like a tank.

I walked on the court and said, "Fellows, they are having classes in that building"—pointing to the school about twenty-five feet away—"your playing is disturbing them."

They looked at each other then looked down at me and said, "Okay."

As they began to leave, I said, "Wait a minute. School is out at three o'clock. I see no reason why you couldn't come back and play ball then. Say about three thirty?"

The smaller of the four players, who seemed to be the leader of the group, said, "We appreciate the offer, but we work the night shift and will be going to work around four."

"Okay, I appreciate your understanding. Thanks for your cooperation." We turned and went our separate ways.

On the last day of the school year, Mrs. Adams walked into my boiler room office. She looked at me and said, in a serious voice, "Mr. Hargis, I want to thank you for handling those black boys that were playing basketball that day. I just really didn't know what I was going to do."

CHRISTMAS LUNCH

To better understand Martha Vaught's principal's fun-loving personality, there were a few events that best describe her. One example was the Christmas luncheon that she served for the faculty each year. Being a good administrator, she would always ask the teachers what they would like for lunch.

She asked, "Mr. Hargis, what would you enjoy for our Christmas lunch?"

I had almost completed one semester in the Metro Nashville school system, and this was the first time anyone had asked my opinion on any subject.

"I think we should have caviar," I jokingly replied.

I had never eaten caviar, or seen caviar, and did not know what it was. I just knew that it was expensive. At the Christmas luncheon sitting in the middle of my plate was a small jar of caviar. I looked over at Mrs. Adams and said, "Thank you," and proceeded to open the jar and spoon out a large bite of caviar. It was the most god-awful-tasting stuff that I had ever put in my mouth. Everyone was watching, and suddenly I realized I was the focal point of the entire faculty. She must have told everyone what she was doing.

I forced myself to swallow and said, "Thank you. This is a real treat. Would anyone like some caviar?"

There was no verbal response from anyone, just smiles. My next statement was a gentleman's way out. "The remainder will be saved for my wife and I to enjoy later."

THE NEW PRINCIPAL

Another incident occurred in late April. Coming to school early, I went by the office but did not see the principal. Instead, there was a blond lady standing with her back to me. Knowing that we sometime had walk-in traffic from the neighborhood, I went to the edge of the door and said, "Excuse me, can I help you?" The lady turned around, looked familiar, but I still could not place her.

Then the lady said, "Mr. Hargis, don't you recognize me?"

"I do now. Your new hairdo threw me off. Going from jet-black to blond was somewhat of a shock. Why did you change your hairstyle?" I replied.

"I just turned fifty and decided that I was going out of middle age with a bang. Come outside and see my new car!"

In the principal's parking space was a brand-new 1966 Ford Galaxy convertible. It was the most beautiful car that I had ever seen, solid black, white top, and red leather interior.

"This is the sharpest car I have ever seen," I said.

She smiled and replied, "Do you think I'm crazy?"

I returned her smile and said, "I like your style,"

Some ten or so years later, I met Mrs. Adams in the central office building. She was walking fast down the hall with a puzzled look on her face. When she saw me, she rushed over and gave me a big hug and said, "Mack, it's good to see you."

She hesitated a moment and said, "You are looking at the dumbest, damn person in this entire school system."

"What in the world are you talking about, Mrs. Adams?"

"I have just come from the retirement office and found out the total of my retirement plus social security exceeds what I am making by over two hundred dollars a month. In other words, I am paying the school system two-hundred-plus dollars a month to work. Yep, I am crazier than hell. This is one problem that I will quickly resolve."

She gave me another quick hug and sped down the hall with a determined look. I never saw her again. She will always be a special lady to me.

GLENDALE PRINCIPAL

The Glendale school principal, Mrs. Little, was completely different from Mrs. Adams, at Martha Vaught. She was a straitlaced, no-nonsense individual but also an effective administrator. When I showed her my schedule change, she looked at it and said, "Good," and nothing else.

I was giving the students the President's Physical Fitness Test. There was a national concern about the physical fitness of our youth, and to address this problem, the government developed a fitness test for schools to administer. While conducting the test, it came to mind that this would be an excellent opportunity to reward students who excelled. I thought a trophy for the winner and runners-up of each grade would be appropriate. All I needed was money for the trophies. Mrs. Little would surely approve the small amount to purchase the trophies.

I made an appointment with Ms. Little to explain my idea. To my amazement and chagrin, Mrs. Little did not agree.

She said, "Mr. Hargis, what about all those other children who will not receive a trophy? Don't you think that will make them feel bad?"

That blew my mind. Without hesitation and mainly without thought my reply was, "Mrs. Little, that is just like communism!"

The next day, my supervisor, the same supervisor who had adjusted my travel schedule, came to see me. I am sure he thought, *Here is a real troublemaker.* This time, we met in the teacher's lounge, much less official than our first meeting. Mrs. Little would not let Mr. Harris use her office.

He sternly looked at me and said, "Explain yourself concerning communism and these trophies."

After my explanation, he smiled and said, "I have a little money in my budget. I might be able to purchase those trophies for you. How much would they cost?"

I told him the approximate price and asked, "What about Mrs. Little?"

He said, "I will talk to her."

Trophies were awarded to the winners of the Presidents Physical Fitness program at the close of school. I had survived my first year, but for some unknown reason, I was transferred to another school the following year.

Litton Junior and Senior High School

Never Say Never

My second year was the start of my life's plan. I was transferred to Litton Junior High School as head coach for the football, girls' basketball, and track teams. My plans for my life never included coaching girls' basketball, but I learned to adjust and make the best of each situation.

When I accepted the position of coaching girls' basketball, my mind went sailing back to my college days. My senior year, I was required to take a seminar course, taught by my basketball coach, Roscoe Williams. The assignment was to develop a program for a high school basketball season. Working diligently on my assignment was pure pleasure as it was something that I was interested in and would use in the future. I submitted my rather lengthy and detailed assignment to Coach Williams at the precise time it was required. He was a stickler for promptness. I felt very good about my report and was expecting an excellent grade.

Much to my surprise and disappointment, my grade was not up to my expectations. The paper was returned with the grade of B. Normally, I did not question teachers or any authority figure about their decisions. That was the way I was raised.

This time, I was very upset and made an exception to normality. I walked into the coach's office without knocking, and I demanded, "Why did you give me a B?"

Coach Williams, a short balding man, turned and looked at me with a side-smile smirk and said, "You did not put anything in your paper about coaching girls' basketball."

Giving a dumbfounding look, I said, "I will never coach girls' basketball!" My first basketball-coaching job was girls' basketball.

I learned a very important lesson: you never say never about your future.

My first-year girls' team had a respectable season and won more games than we lost. The following two years of my three-year tenure at Litton Junior High School, we won the league championship. Our success was due to the hard work and dedication of the girls and by opening the gymnasium on Saturday. The girls would voluntarily come to practice on Saturday. They were a great group of girls. When I pause to think about my professional career, coaching these girls' rates at the top of my list of enjoyable times.

There were several instances involving these girls that remain vividly in my mind. I purchased a Volkswagen camper for the primary purpose of carrying the basketball team to and from the games. I would pack five or six girls in the van, and a parent would bring the remainder of the players. Generally, the girls were laughing and joking on the way to and from the games. This particular game was with our major rival.

We won the game by a small margin but while the battle on the basketball court was raging Mother Nature was doing a little raging of her own. Walking out of the gym, we found a coat of ice on everything. We chipped the ice away from the doors of the camper and finally crawled inside. I cranked the engine and turned on the defroster to melt the ice from the windshield. Volkswagen heaters were notorious for being pitifully inadequate, so the windshields remained iced over. Fortunately, I had an ice scraper and managed to clear the ice from the windshield. The girls were elated about winning the game and the possibility of being out of school the next day due to the weather. These two items caused a lot of adrenaline-induced excitement. It never occurred to these teenage girls that the drive home could be treacherous. My main concern was a steep hill that we had to negotiate.

As we slowly drove from the parking lot, the girls were laughing, hollering, and singing all at the same time. I was trying to concentrate on the slick pavement and deplored the noise coming from the back of the bus. The noise was not increasing my concentration level. At this particular time, I did not feel it would be prudent to ask the girls to be quiet and keep their joy inside. Bringing their attention to our icy situation would only increase my and their anxiety. I managed to ignore their celebration as we inched closer to the hill. Slowing to a crawl, we started down the crest of the hill. The streetlights reflected an eerie glow from the ice covered the road. The camper was in second gear and moving slowly on the icy asphalt.

We crept down the hill as the tires were desperately trying to gain traction from the small amount of snow that had dusted the ice. Halfway down the hill, the tires suddenly gave up their grip and submitted to the control of the ice.

The front began sliding to the left while the rear of the camper slowly moved to the right. I turned the steering wheel, trying to correct for our skid, but to very little avail. As we begin to slide sideways down the hill, the players became deathly silent. The girls had realized the situation. As we slid sideways down the hill, we were unrelentingly moving toward the three-foot-deep ditch on left side of the road. Slightly turning the steering wheel allowed the tires to gain some traction on the snow and modestly corrected our slide to impending doom.

By this time, the girls had assessed our precarious situation and were fully aware of the danger. I had no trouble concentrating as their joyous celebration had come to a screeching halt. There was not a peep coming from the rear of the camper.

Suddenly the deathly silence turned into squeals and screams as the left front tire struck the shoulder of the road, causing a sudden jerk only inches from the ditch. There was enough gravel on the shoulder of the road to stop the slide that caused the camper rear to slip forward and become the front. We were sliding down the center of the road backward. No sooner than we were aware of our new situation, the vehicle started another circle. We were slowly gaining speed down the hill and were definitely out of control. By the time we reached the bottom of the hill, the van had corrected itself, and we were pointed in the right direction. In addition, we were on the correct side of the road. I carefully applied the brakes and slowed to a controllable speed.

I asked, "Is everyone okay back there?"

Still, there was dead silence.

Then finally one of the more adventurous girls said in a loud voice, "That was fun! Let's do it again."

After a short delay, there were several replies such as "Yeah, right!" and "You crazy?"

Rather than going back to school and causing the parents to drive on the slick roads, I carried each player to their house. After depositing the players, I begin to relive the situation. On my way home, the more my thoughts went to what might have happened, the weaker my knees became, along with intense nausea.

Coaching these girls taught me two major things: Dedicated players will reach their goals, and these ladies were conscientious. They would cry if they lost and cry if they won. The same emotion just caused by a different stimulus. It took me half a season to learn the difference. Those were wonderful girls and great times.

After three successful years at Litton Junior, which included two girls' basketball championships and a Nashville citywide track championship, I was transferred to Litton High School and became the assistant boys' basketball coach. I remained in this position for three years. Each year at the end of unsuccessful basketball seasons, the head coach would tell me he was giving up the team, and it would be all mine next year. That gave me hope and excitement, but that never happened. At the beginning of each year, he would continue as head coach. I was waiting patiently, well, not patiently, but waiting each year for a head coaching opportunity.

Front row: Terry Hester, Pam Brown, *Managers. Back row:* Mary Sue Meador, Helen Jean Hollis, Kathy Hooper, Melinda Hoffman, Darlene Lawson, Gayle Adams, Elaine Ferrell, Jackie Henley, Becky Murphy, Kathy Frye, Debbie Garretty, Jane McGinnis.

Isaac Litton Junior High Basketball Champions 1967

First row: Gail Adams, Patsy Parker, Brenda Wheeler, Ellen Echols, Elaine Ferrell. *Second row:* Ava Walker, Dottie Shanks, Bettye Ann Sadler, Kathy Watson, Dawn Stewart, Debra Bumpus. *Third row:* Debra Kelley, Connie Griggs, Virginia Blackman, Laura Register, Kathy Cornett, Janice Taylor, Diane Felts.

Isaac Litton Junior High Basketball Champions 1968

Litton Junior High City Track Champions 1966
Front row: David Temple, Second row: Lynn Ballou, Buddy Harper
Back row: Bob Galloway, Johnny Blankenship, Bob Sanford

LITTON AUTO ENGINE PROJECT

At Litton Junior, I was assigned to teach three classes of general science. A chapter that I always enjoyed teaching was the internal combustion engine. My father-in-law, Abe Fesmire, was an auto mechanic, and while working with him in his shop, he taught me the basics of the gas engine. I tried to impart my excitement and on the job learning experience to my mostly unconcerned students.

It was in the spring of the year, and I was coaching the track team. After practice, I noticed a truck backed up to the school's boiler room. There was nothing in the room worth stealing, so what in the world is going on? Making a beeline to the truck, I closed in on the action. I saw the head custodian in the front seat of an old 1946 suet-black Dodge pickup. Approaching the truck, I said, "Hey, Mr. Simms, what are you doing? You need any help?"

"Just throwing this old motor in the boiler room until I can take it to the dump" was his reply.

"What's wrong with the motor?"

"Well, I bought this engine sight unseen, thinking I was getting a real deal, but you know how good deals usually turn out."

"What is wrong with it?"

"Take a close look at the right side of the block. There is a big hole where a piston rod went through. I paid fifty dollars for that motor, and it is junk. Darn it! I will never learn!"

I began to think, which is dangerous for me, to say the least, and said, "What will you take for the old engine?"

"Take for it, I'll give it to you just so I don't have to carry it to the junkyard."

"Okay, I will take it if you will let me keep it in the boiler room for a few days."

"You got it and keep in there as long as you like."

What am I going to do with this old-shot motor? Simple. It was going to become my internal combustion engine visual teaching aid. For the next two weeks after school and on weekends, I and a couple of students dissembled and cleaned the engine.

This cleaning process involved a cleaning solution called "Gunk" and wire brushes. For several hours, we would spray, brush, rinse, and start over. Finally, the engine turned from a greasy, black, sticky, mess to a metallic gray. All clean parts were coated with a light-gray rust-proof paint. Spare parts from my father-in-law's garage replaced the parts of the engine that were damaged.

I was not sure how I was going to use it in my classroom until my principal, Mr. Smith, discovered what I was doing. He came by my room and suggested that I call the science supervisor and ask for an instructional motor stand.

He said, "Be sure you ask for an 'instructional' motor stand. It sounds much more educational, and you will be more likely to get it."

I said, "Okay, I can do that."

Within two weeks, we were the proud owners of an "instructional" motor stand, and my new instructional aid was ready. As we started the chapter on the internal combustion engine, I explained the functions of the four-stroke engine using the newly painted engine bolted securely to the instructional motor stand. I disassembled the engine in front of class and answered any questions. Then the class was divided into pairs. The instructional engine was rolled to the room across the hall.

Each pair of students was given the necessary tools to disassemble and reassemble the motor. This continued for two weeks until each student had learned the function of the automobile engine, both academically and mechanically. All students were required to accomplish this procedure.

The next year, I was transferred to another school. I have often wondered what happened to that old "instructional motor and stand."

Litton Marquee

SMOKING STALL

My life's plan was moving steadily forward. I had just been promoted to Litton High School as the assistant football and basketball coach. Success at the junior high with two basketball championships and a citywide track champion must have pleased the powers in charge enough to boost me to the high school sports program. I was pleased and proud.

Isaac Litton High School was built in the early 1930s and was not the most up-to-date building in the school system. The old hardwood floors were covered with green and light-gray asbestos tiles. In the 1930s, the hardwood floors were lightly covered with an oil to keep the dust down. On a damp, hot day, in some areas of the building, a person could detect a slight petroleum odor.

There was no air-conditioning in the school, and during early fall and late spring, classrooms turned into a hotbox with temperatures reaching the high eighties. The winter was worse with the steam heating system. Radiators were located below the windows, which allowed the heat to squirt outside through leaks around the window frames. I always wondered why radiators were located under the windows. It appeared that if they were on the interior wall, the heat would warm people as it moved to escape through the windows. The building was old and had a lot of quirks, but I dearly loved that old building. Walking into the school each morning was akin to stepping back in history.

My assignment was to teach United States history. I was replacing Mrs. Alice Cassetty.

She had been a mainstay at Litton for years. Her desk looked as if she had just walked away for a few minutes. Everything was still in order. She had taken nothing with her. On her desk was a fancy stapler, a bucketload of pens and pencils, four silver dimes, and a photograph of George Washington. The item that I am sure she mostly treasured was the autographed picture of George Washington. It was an eight-by-ten black-and-white glossy picture of President Washington with a note written at the bottom right corner.

After fifty years, I can still remember the quote:

To my favorite and best teacher.

Love,
George

Most coaches had last-period planning. This would allow them to be in a dressing room before the players arrived for practice. This fine fall day, I was heading to the dressing room about fifteen minutes before the final bell. I was silently and swiftly moving down the hall. The principal's office was on the right, and four steps down the hall on the left was the downstairs boys' restroom. As I passed the restroom, there was a loud *kaboom*! I stopped, hesitated momentarily to determine exactly what and from where the noise came. While quickly scanning the area, I noticed a stream of white vapor slowly moving along the top of the boys' restroom door. The white vapor was followed by a blackish smoke and pungent odor of gunpowder.

Just as I reached the door, it burst open with such force that one of the three hinges broke loose. In front of me was a young man lunging out of the bathroom with a bewildered look and eyes that appeared the size of saucers. Smoke was bellowing from around his head and shoulders. His left hand was still pushing on the door while his right hand held his pants that were hanging around his knees.

I pushed him back in the restroom and said, "Get back in there. Get dressed!"

He made a grunting noise, "Gugg, gugg," and again lunged forward to the hall.

This time, I grabbed him, dragged him back inside the restroom, and said, "Calm down and get your pants up." I did notice through the smoke a large brown spot in the seat of his white underwear.

Smoke was thick with the foul stench of gunpowder, and there were pieces of white material scattered over the floor. By the time the student had pulled up his pants, both the principal and assistant principal appeared through the smoke. The principal hollowed, "What happened? Is anyone hurt?"

While still holding the student, I told the principal, "This young man was trying to get out of restroom right after the explosion."

The principal told the young man, "Come with me."

Before I let the student go, I checked to see if he had pulled up his pants satisfactorily and told the principal, "I don't think he was involved in this stunt."

As the student entered the less smoky hallway, I noticed the brown underwear spot had bled through to his pants. This incident made me late to football practice, but that was not a concern as we were having a skull session. I told my smoky bathroom story to the coaches. They all listened with a chuckle or two and a concern that the student may have been injured.

Early the following day, I saw Mr. Smith, the principal, in the cafeteria sipping his first on-the-job cup of coffee. I strolled over and asked if he had solved the big bang episode.

He smiled, took another sip of coffee, and said, "Not solved yet but better understood."

That answer only piqued my interest more.

"Hope you don't mind me asking what does that mean?"

He took another a sip of coffee while lovingly cradling his cup. He did enjoy his coffee. "The young man you apprehended is innocent. He was a victim of being in the wrong place at the wrong time. He was in the restroom for legitimate reasons."

"What about the explosion?"

He continued, "Bob, the student you caught had just entered the toilet stall to take care of an urgent call from Mother Nature. Just as he had dropped his pants and started squatting down on the toilet seat, a large boom and a flash of light erupted all around him. He did not know what had happened.

"He told me, 'I thought the whole school had blown up and was on fire. I wanted out of there fast. I opened the door and started out. That is when Coach Hargis pushed me back into the restroom. I was scared and started out again, and this time, Coach grabbed me and pulled me into the restroom and told me to pull up my pants.'"

"Yeah, that's right. What caused the explosion?" I asked.

The coffee cup was near the empty mark and needed a refill. As the principal poured his second cup, he said, "After investigating the restroom, it appeared that someone had set a time bomb behind the toilet Bob was going to use."

"Time bomb?"

"Yeah, you know about those. Students go into the restroom for a quick smoke and use the cigarette butt as a time delay fuse. One of those large cherry bombs is used for the explosive device. While the cigarette is still burning, they place it behind the toilet and lay the cherry bomb fuse across the unburned cigarette. When the burning cigarette reaches the cherry bomb fuse, you have a big *kaboom*."

"I have heard about that, but there was a lot smoke for one cherry bomb."

"Right. Sometime they will put two cherry bombs on the cigarette fuse, or occasionally, they will come up with one of those old two-inch red firecrackers. You can't buy the big red ones today because they are too dangerous and powerful. Occasionally, a student will find one."

"I remember those. A fellow in my hometown blew two fingers off fooling with them."

As the principal moved to the door with a full cup of fresh coffee, he motioned for me to follow. I refilled my cup and walked with him. He was about five feet eight inches tall with thinning hair. Mr. Smith was the former coach of a football Clinic Bowl City Championship team and state basketball championship to his credit. He was well respected.

"There are times the rascals will put a small piece of cardboard over the bomb and a cigarette to reduce the possibility of the bomb being found. I think that happened here. This explosion had to be at least two cherry bombs or maybe a big red and a cherry bomb. There was a lot of smoke and damage."

"What was the white material I saw all over the floor when I opened the window to let the smoke out? There was so much smoke I could barely make it out and even stumbled over a larger piece."

Mr. Smith continued, "The toilet was blown completely of the base and broke into a hundred pieces. That was what you stumbled over."

"It's a wonder Bob was not hurt."

"I suggested his parents take him to the doctor and have his hearing checked," replied Mr. Smith.

To my knowledge, the culprit was never apprehended. Bob suffered no long-term health problems, at least not physical. I have often wondered if he checks behind the toilets, even today, before using them. Or maybe has cold chills bounce around on his spine from flashbacks *whenever* he considers entering a booth.

My third year at Litton, 1971, was the year the federal court intervened and turned my hopeful expectations upside down. The court order phased out Litton and sent the faculty and students in four different directions. My transfer was to McGavock High School, the largest school in the state as an assistant football and basketball coach.

McGavock Comprehensive High School

ARE WE ON THE SAME PAGE

Most everyone feels sorry for a person or group that has been mistreated. If the maltreatment has been well publicized or is commonly known, the victims may receive preferential treatment. At times, this was true during the school integration process.

There were some teachers and administrators who thought they were helping black students by allowing them to slide academically and on school rules. In reality, these educators were ensuring later life failure for these individuals. Their hearts were in the right place, but in my opinion, their methods were in complete error.

One school rule during the early 1970s was that students were not to wear hats in the building. I'm not sure why this rule was instated; I assume it was the Southern custom that a man should not wear a hat in the house. This was the dictum that caused more trouble and accomplished less than any that I have ever known. We enforced it because it was a rule.

As I was returning to class after lunch, I rounded the corner, and there, right in front of me, stood a student with his hat boldly cocked sideways on his head. There was no ignoring this situation because many students were watching.

As the young man came toward me, I said, "Please remove your hat."

He looked my way, made no comment, and began to move past me without making any effort to comply. I took a step toward him and removed his prize from his head as he walked by.

He stopped, whirled around, angrily looked at me, and said, "Hey, man, gimme my hat."

I did not answer him, just turned, and walked toward the nearest principal's office.

The student ran around in front of me, hollering, "Gimme my hat" as he chest-bumped me while grabbing for it. I kept the hat out of his reach and remained silent.

I got to the office, walked past the secretary's desk, and pitched the hat on the principal's desk, and said, "He was wearing this hat in the cafeteria." I said nothing else, left his office, and headed upstairs to my classroom.

After class was over, I went into the restroom adjacent to my classroom and conducted my potty-duty assignment. Finding the restroom with no problems, I assumed my position as a hall monitor. Looking down the corridor, I was surprised to see the student that I had decapped in the cafeteria. He was exiting a classroom with that same hat cocked sideways on his head. My first thought was to confiscate it again.

After taking two steps, I returned to my hall duty post. I thought, *Why should I go through the physical and verbal abuse again when the rules did not seem to matter for this particular individual or his principal?*

Recently, a former McGavock teacher and I had lunch, and he told me of his experience that occurred forty years ago. This incident was still firmly entrenched in his mind and helped develop his educational philosophy of firm but fair on his road to becoming a superintendent.

He was in the hall at McGavock when a black student ran past him. From around the corner and ten steps behind came an administrator chasing him. The administrator was huffing and puffing and said, "That fellow stole a purse. Catch him!" The teacher was young and, knowing the school building, used a shortcut and caught the student just as he was exiting a back door. He apprehended the student and brought him to the administrator that had been chasing him.

Being a young teacher and directed to accomplish a task by his boss, he proudly said, "Here is your man. Got him just as he was leaving the building."

The administrator said, "Thank you. I'll take it from here."

The next day, the apprehending teacher saw the same young man walking down the hall during classes. Rather than talking with the student, the teacher went directly to the administrator and asked, "What is that student I caught for you yesterday doing in school today? You told me he had been caught stealing. What's he doing here?"

The administrator said, "Well, he is poor and doesn't have much, so I talked to him about right and wrong. He promised he would go to class and not steal again."

The red-faced teacher said, "I just saw him in the hall, and it is obvious that he is skipping class. Don't you ever ask me to run down one of your boys again if you are just going to let them go."

I'm sure those administrators thought they were doing what was best for those students. For those who were trying to follow the rules set forth, it was very demoralizing, knowing a silent double standard existed.

African Dance Troupe

During the early 1970s, integration of the black and white schools in Nashville was the focal point of the entire city. Two cultures were forced to combine in a short period with very little money provided from the federal or state governments for training and implementing this court order. There were a few activities planned by local administrators and consulting college sociologists. These programs generally consisted of in-service for school faculties. The in-service programs became known as hand-holding and singing. We were all encouraged to read a book by Dr. Thomas Anthony Harris, *I Am Ok—You're Ok.* I have always believed the reason there was little training prior to the implementation of the court order was the lack of time more than money. Another probably more important reason was that this type of forced merger had never been done before. No one had any experience in forcibly combining two cultures.

With the above background, the forthcoming incident was one that was embedded in a lack of communication, which resulted in an ill-fated decision. Each Thursday, there was an administrative meeting at McGavock to plan activities for the next week. The executive principal brought before his assistants a request he had received concerning hosting an African dance troupe. The dancers would perform before the student body.

He said, "I have talked with the officials at Tennessee State University, principal at Overton High School and others who have seen the dance troupe perform, and they all said it was a positive experience."

With those glowing recommendations and the prevailing atmosphere of trying to help white students better understand black culture, a date was set for their performance.

McGavock High School had an excellent auditorium with professional stage lighting that was the envy of all performing arts schools. The only negative was the auditorium accommodated six hundred students, and the school had an enrollment of three thousand. With this limitation, only one-fourth of the student body could view an assembly program. To treat everyone fairly, a rotating schedule was devised so that each small school had the opportunity to see an assembly program. Those students not scheduled for the assembly reported to their homeroom.

The day came for the assembly program, and the executive principal explained on the intercom, "Students, we are very fortunate to have a world-acclaimed African dance troupe perform for us today. I know everyone will enjoy the performance."

With that introduction, one-fourth of the student body was ushered into the auditorium. Students were seated and again told how fortunate they were to see these world-renowned African dancers.

After the verbal preparation was completed, the curtains slowly opened, and eight African dancers appeared in brightly colored costumes. As they gracefully moved around the stage, their costumes flowing behind them gave the impression of eight butterflies effortlessly floating through the air. After the first act, the performers received a warm applause from students and teachers.

As the curtain opened for the second act, their costumes had changed considerably. The dancers were topless. There was a unison gasp from the audience and then complete silence. Approximately half of the student body had their hands covering their mouths in utter surprise and shock. The other half was studying the dance moves with renewed interest. This surprise shocked the executive principal who was leaning against the back wall of the auditorium, watching the performance. As the dancers appeared bare-chested, gracefully moving through their performance, the executive principal began slowly sliding down the wall in total disbelief. I'm sure his mind was racing with thoughts about what he should do. Fortunately, the second act was not exceptionally long, and no action from the executive principal was the best action to take, which he performed flawlessly.

This was before cell phones were in existence. McGavock High School was well supplied with pay phones throughout the building. As soon as the program was completed, the students were dismissed to their next class. This gave them ample opportunity to seek out every pay phone in the building. Most were in use, by girls that attended the assembly; they were calling their parents to report this offensive experience they had to endure.

These Southern-born and Southern-bred parents began calling the school to express their outrage of exposing their children to such filth. And not surprisingly, in a short time, the school was a beehive of activity. The news media seemed to be in every square foot of the building, trying to interview students, teachers, and administrators. TV, radio, newspaper reporters and one locally published magazine editor appeared. Never, to my knowledge, have sixteen bare breasts caused so much media excitement.

As in all media-induced excitement, the bare-breasted African dance troupe intrigue faded into history like a vapor swept away by the wind. Even though the media calmed their pursuit of this story, the other principals in the Nashville school system did not. The executive principal received from his peers and, to somewhat a lesser degree, the assistant principals an ungodly amount of ribbing.

I feel sure the institutions that recommended the dancers had not seen the bare-breasted segment of the performance, and only McGavock School saw this portion of their program.

At any rate, the incident was best described by a teacher when he said, "As I sat there observing this performance, it was almost as if I were watching pages of the *National Geographic Magazine* come to life right before my eyes."

THE KNIFE FIGHT AND
THE LEAPING KING

McGavock High School was formed by the consolidation of three schools. None of the students from the three schools wanted to be at McGavock. Cameron High School, an all-black school with a proud history, had won the state basketball championship for several years; Donelson High and Two Rivers were mostly white, strong rivals, and located less than six miles apart. This mixture was not destined for a smooth ride.

I was transferred to McGavock and assigned to teach tenth-grade health. My classroom was adjacent to a boys' restroom. One of my assignments was to monitor the restroom between each class. A few restrooms were not located close to a classroom, and without teacher supervision, students had some of their possessions taken. The general mode of operation was for two or more students to band together between classes and gang up on the innocent student who was in the restroom for legitimate reason. Once the student victim went into the restroom, one of the band of thieves would turn the lights off, and the others would take everything he had—backpack, watches, billfold, change, and sometimes lunch tickets. The victim could not identify any of the thieves because there were no windows, and the lights were out.

To alleviate the situation, the administration assigned teachers to monitor the restroom near them. This assignment became known as potty duty. Once the thieves realized that a teacher was going to be close, the stealing became less frequent. Sometimes a teacher could not be on duty due to other obligation, and problems would redevelop. The administration finally decided to wire the lights switches direct, which caused the lights to remain on at all times. This slowed the restroom crime rate to a crawl.

Teachers stood by their classroom door during class changes, a standard operating procedure in most high schools. Each day, I would come from the classroom to my potty post, enter the restroom, and sometimes find a student lighting up a cigarette or possibly a joint and send these individuals to the principal's office. On this particular day, while performing potty duty, I heard a loud commotion coming from down the hall. I immediately went to the scene and saw a group of students encircling another student lying on the floor. This ring of students was staring in disbelief of what was taking place. Girls were screaming and running down the hall. Other students were yelling, "Find a teacher! Find a teacher!"

I pushed through the group and found four black students kicking a white student. These kicks were not playful jabs; the force could have easily made a fifty-yard-field goal. When the kicking students saw me, they ran down the hall.

My main concern was the student on the floor with blood coming from his nose, ears, and mouth. He had managed to get to his knees when the attack stopped and was recklessly swinging a six-inch blade knife. It appeared his vision was impaired because he was jabbing his knife at anything that moved. I came from behind him and grabbed his arm to control the knife. I lifted him off his feet, pushed him back to the floor as I loudly barked, "I'm a teacher! I'm a teacher!"

Just as I had maintained control of the knife-swinging student, a shadow came zipping over the top of me. My first thought was that those kicking devils were back, and I would be their next field goal attempt. I looked up from my kneeling position, preparing to protect myself when I saw the soles of two shoes about four feet in the air and sailing over the left side of my head. It was Bob King! Bob was the computer teacher, in his twenties, and physically well built. He had heard the commotion and came to see what he could do to help. The kicking students ran down the hall with Bob in hot pursuit. I have often wondered how far he jumped. He leaped at least ten feet and cleared my head by a foot or more.

Knowing the escaping students were being pursued, I picked up the injured student, retrieved the knife, and carried him to the nearest principal's office. Since the principal was not there, I took the student into the inner office, sat him down, pitched the knife on the desk, and ask the secretary for water and towels. She was way ahead of me. A student office worker appeared with water and towels. I began to clean blood from the student's face and check his injuries. Before I could finish my face-cleaning task, the tardy bell rang.

The secretary and guidance counselor were watching and said, "We will take care of him. You can go back to class."

They were right. I needed to be in class as this type of commotion sometimes escalated into larger problems. Fortunately, that was not the case with this incident.

I do not know what started the conflict or the resolution. I did find out that two of the students were twins and well known for causing trouble. Even now, some fifty years later, when I close my eyes and think about McGavock, I can still see Bob King leaping over me in pursuit of those violent students. I will always appreciate him.

SKEETER SUCCEEDS

The year was 1971, a troubled time for the educational system in Nashville. In 1954, the NAACP had sued the Nashville Board of Education for equal opportunity, and the lawsuit had finally come to a conclusion. The school system was legally bound to allow black students to attend schools with white students. Due to the demographics of the communities, the only way to implement the court order in the time allowed was through a plan called *busing*.

School buses were used to take students out of their neighborhoods to schools in other areas of town. Both black and white students' schools lives and communities were put into turbulent disruption, which led to conflicts both physical and social. The rapidly forced implementation of this desegregation plan was destined for problems.

The plan of integrating black and white students was the brainchild of Dr. James Coleman, sociologist from the University of Chicago. In 1974, four years after implementing his plan, Dr. Coleman admitted that the experimental busing for integration purposes was a failure. Even after the author of the program admitted this was a failure, the die was cast, and busing continued even to this day. Everyone was caught up in this whirlwind of negativity that invaded Nashville.

Isaac Litton High School, where I was teaching and coaching, was phased out. The students attending Litton were rezoned to several different high schools. The previous plan was to have the students attend the school closest to them, which allowed both black and white students to attend their community schools. This had taken place at Litton High School and worked relatively well. Apparently, this was not fast enough for the federal judge. I, like all the students and teachers at Litton, was sent to a new location.

I was assigned to McGavock High School, a new comprehensive high school that was absorbing three community schools, two white and one black. The school's enrollment was three thousand.

I assumed my duties as an assistant football coach. With three seasoned football teams coming together, everyone was predicting a championship team. With three people vying for each position and very little time to determine whose skills best fit each position, we could not accomplish what everyone expected. This led to disappointments and morale disillusionment. The following several years, McGavock's football teams did have some success but never reached the potential that was expected. Basketball was a different situation. There was more time to prepare for the upcoming season. The head basketball coach, Joe Allen, had already distinguished himself by winning the state championship in 1964 while coaching at Donelson.

His physical appearance would not indicate prowess in the sport of basketball. He was approximately five feet ten inches tall, average build, and low-key approach to most everything. He was obviously a strong student of the game of basketball and player psychology.

The other assistant coach, Gene Speight, was black, tall, slender, and young, In the 1970s, the favorite hairstyle for blacks was known as the Afro. They would allow their hair to grow long and then tease it so that it would stand out. Due to the curliness of the hair, the Afro style would hold form and could add two or three inches of height. Gene had an excellent Afro. With one-and-a-half- to two-inch heels on shoes, which were also stylish at the time, and his three-inch Afro, Gene presented an impressive sight. He was basketball knowledgeable and had a similar low-key approach as Joe Allen.

When time came for tryout for the boys' basketball team, Coach Allen met with Gene and me to outline the procedure for evaluating the players. We agreed to run the players through drills and watch three-on-three games. As players were evaluated, each coach would write down names of those individuals he felt had the skills to make the team. This was really a sad time for me as I looked around and saw at least a hundred players trying out for the team. There were too many participants and too few slots. Many of the students had athletic ability to play in smaller schools. Combining three schools resulting in a student body of three thousand, the players abilities had to be exceptional to make the team. We were aware of this problem and made sure everyone got a fair and equal opportunity.

Coach Allen was bald, his head was as slick as glass, and he wore a well-designed toupee. Most people knew he wore a hairpiece and thought nothing about it, but he did not wear his hairpiece during basketball practice.

The next-day following tryouts, Coach Allen called Gene and me into his office, which was a converted storage closet.

He was smiling and said, "I got to tell you what happened today."

Pointing to a slender young player under the goal, Joe said, "See that kid? His name is Robert Williams. He is in my third-period math class. Robert came to me before class today and ask why I was not at basketball practice yesterday. Robert said, 'Coach Allen, how can you coach a team and not be at practice? There was a bald-headed man coaching, but I did not see you."

Joe just smiled and did not reply. He raised the edge of his hairpiece so that Robert could see he was the bald man at practice.

Robert's reply was "Oh" and returned to his seat.

We enjoyed a laugh at Robert's nonacademic education. A person learns many things at school that are not in the textbook.

After the tryouts were completed, we took our notes, sat down around Coach Allen's desk, and started discussing players. Considering the large number of students trying out for the team, I was pleased that we had generally come to the same consensus. There was one player that I was interested in that Coach Speight and Allen did not have on their list.

The individual that I thought had promise was a tall, skinny black kid that was six feet, three inches tall and had an arm span of six and one-half feet. He was so skinny that some people said, "If he stuck his tongue out and turned sideways, he would look like a zipper."

His slim body and long arms had acquired him the street name of Skeeter. I assumed it was because some of his peers thought he looked like a mosquito. His moves were rather slow and sluggish during the tryout, and he was sweating profusely. While he was wait-ing his turn for the next drill, I approached him and said, "Are you feeling all right?"

He stepped out of line and said, "I guess so. I have been in the bed with the flu for the three days, but I just couldn't miss tryouts."

I told him, "Go get some water and don't overdo it."

My thoughts were, *This kid really loves basketball and has a lot of guts.*

When Skeeter's name did not appear on Joe or Gene's list, I suggested we give him a try, especially since he came off a flu bed to be there. I was trying to think fast enough to counter the rebuttal I was sure would come.

Coach Allen looked at Gene and said, "Mack, I've got no prob-lem with giving him a shot if Gene doesn't."

Gene said, "Let's see what skinny Skeeter can do."

That set the tone for our relationship. We would always discuss situations before we made a decision, except during the heat of the game that was Coach Allen's call.

Skeeter was one of my life's better decisions. He recovered from the flu and became our number six man that year and played in the state tournament the following years. His skill on the court improved and impressed me enough that I decided to go to bat for him again.

Having played college basketball and maintaining contact with my college coach, I decided to tell him about Skeeter.

The phone was answered, "Athletic department, Coach Bray speaking."

"Hello, Coach, this is Mack Hargis. How are you doing?"

We discussed a few old times for a minute, and then Coach Bray suddenly said, "Mack, I got a class waiting. Anything I can help you with?"

"Well, Coach, I might be able to help you. Do you have all your scholarships filled?"

Coach Bray said, "Hold on a minute."

I could hear him tell one of his assistants, "Tell the class I will be there shortly. Huh? Well, would you mind teaching them today? I need to finish this phone call."

"Okay, Coach," I heard the assistant reply.

"Mack? Mack, you still on the line?"

"Yeah, I am still here."

Coach Bray said with renewed interest, "Now tell me about this player of yours."

"I think we have a sleeper for you. He has done a good job this year, is a solid no-showboat player, and a good student."

"If you think that much of him, let's set up a tryout. I will get a date for him to come down. I am sure Saturday would be best."

Coach Allen was informed of my conservation with Coach Bray and the tryout that had been arranged. I asked Skeeter if he needed transportation to Lambuth University, which was about a hundred miles away. He told me he had transportation.

Sketter earned a four-year scholarship and a degree in business administration.

After Skeeter's graduation, Coach Bray called and said, "If you have any more players like Vincent Harvell, send them to me. I also wanted you to know that Vincent has a good job with the state."

Skeeter was working for the Tennessee State Banking division as an auditor. A year or two later, I heard that he had bought a house and moved his mother out of the projects. Vincent was a hard worker and a good person.

Even though it has been over forty-five years ago, I remember falling victim to the flu shortly after basketball tryouts. I have often wondered if Skeeter gave it to me.

A SMALL SCHOOL PRINCIPAL MISTAKE

The federal court order had managed to reduce the number of high schools in Nashville by approximately half. Suddenly 50 percent of the high school coaches in Nashville were out of work. The school system managed to keep from laying off anyone, but many did not have the job they preferred. I realized that my chance of obtaining a high school head coaching position in the next few years was as likely as winning the lottery. I began to look at other options.

A small school principal position became available at McGavock High School, and I applied for it. McGavock was divided by alphabet into four sections with one principal per section. Each section was called a small school. Educationally speaking, it was known as a "School Within a School Concept." Fortunately, or unfortunately depending on how you look at it, I got the job. It was the middle of the basketball season, and I was serving as assistant basketball coach when I was assigned the principalship. It was decided that I would remain with the basketball team for the remainder of the year and give up coaching duties the following year.

The next game following my appointment was with North High School, which was predominantly black. Both black and white communities were upset with the court-ordered school desegregation, which caused a constant uneasiness. One could feel the tension when entering the gymnasium. There were several police officers assigned to maintain order. The seats were full with standing room only. If things got out of control, it could be a volatile situation.

The persons who were really in charge for maintaining order were the basketball officials, and they were well aware of their responsibility. They blew their whistles loudly, shouted directions to the players in a snappy, authoritative manner, and were looking for any reason to show everyone that they were in control.

Unfortunately for me, I gave them this opportunity, and they took full advantage of it. Early in the first half, a scuffle for the ball took place in front of the McGavock bench. It was at my feet; I could see everything. The whistle blew, and the official pointed to North's end of the court, signaling North's ball. This was not right! This infraction happened six inches in front of me. The North player touched the ball just as it went out of bounds. I slapped my hands together, raised off the bench about six inches, and immediately sat down. Before my bottom hit the bench, I knew I had made a big mistake, a big, big mistake!

By the time I sat down on the bench, which could have been measured in milliseconds, I had a big hairy finger pointing at me, hollering so the entire gym could hear, "Technical foul on you!"

I wanted so badly to jump up and tell him he was wrong. Better judgment prevailed as I looked straight at him, just shook my head and didn't say a word. You don't argue with the zebra-striped individuals with whistles, even if they are wrong. They are never wrong—I must remember that.

I am sure individuals who assigned me to an administrative position must have been having second thoughts. My first day on the job as a principal, and I lost my cool. Principals are supposed to handle explosives situations with calmness and finesse. We won, so my mistake did not affect the outcome of the game. The next day, there were no comments about my technical foul—at least not to me. It was really embarrassing.

THE McGAVOCK ROSE

Since the beginning of organized schooling, from the one-room schoolhouse to the large schools of today, students have aided teachers and administrators. There is no way that a school can operate smoothly without student help. Most of the students that work in the office are exceptional in their academic work. On occasions, in order to give us a better opportunity to encourage them, we would allow students who were having difficulty to work in the office.

One such student was Rose. We called her Rosie. She was about five feet, two inches tall, always had a smile on her face, big brown eyes, and was cute as a button. Rosie was a good worker and would accomplish almost any task we ask of her. Her grades were poor, but I always thought that was because she did not study. She worked in the office, and our main goal was to help her improve her vocabulary.

When using the word vocabulary, I'm actually talking about profanity. In normal conversation, Rosie would roll out phrases and words that would make a sailor blush. While in the office, if she came out with profanity, the secretary, guidance counselor, or anyone that heard it would correct her. If a VIP came to our office and Rosie was working, we made sure to send her on an errand. I remember two cases in points when the governor toured the school, and later that month, the mayor attended a program. A line of news media, print, and TV followed both politicians. If Rosie had been there, I'm sure she would have given the media something to report.

After about a month of Rosie working in the office and very little progress being made on vocabulary improvement, it was time to increase pressure. We decided to call her mother to enlist her help in improving Rosie's conversation skills.

I asked Rosie to come into my office and said, "Rosie, your language is not improving. You are still using a lot of curse words."

Rosie sat there and did not say a word. She just lowered her head slightly to the right and looked at me out of the corners of her big brown eyes.

"I don't want to suspend you, so the only thing left for me to do is call your mother."

I could tell Rosie didn't like the idea by the look she gave me. Her nose wrinkled, eyes squinted, and she was gritting her teeth, but she did not ask me not to call her.

Picking up the phone, I asked, "Rosie, what is your phone number?"

She reluctantly said after a moment's hesitation, "262-4321." I dialed the numbers, and her mother answered.

"Mrs. James, this is Mack Hargis, Rosie's principal. I am calling to ask your help with Rosie."

Her mother, in a rather strained and semiexcited voice, said, "What kind of problem you having with Rosie?"

"When Rosie opens her mouth, mostly profanity rolls out. Her verbal behavior is getting out of hand, and it can't be tolerated at school. If she does not stop cursing, we will have to send her home."

Rosie's mother, in an irritated voice, said, "We will certainly get that stopped right now. Put her on the phone!"

I was talking on my inner-office phone that had an extension in the outer office.

I told Rosie, "Your mother wants to speak with you. Go to the front office phone and talk with her."

I stayed on my phone to listen and to give any input that her mother might need from me.

Apparently, Rosie's mother did not know that I was listening on the extension.

She said, "Rosie, what in the hell are you doing cussing at school? You know damn well that you ain't supposed to go there cussing, and if you don't stop that shit, when you get home, I will beat your frigging ass. Goddamn it, you quit cussing at school, and I don't want to hear anything else from that damn, dumb ass principal."

It was one of those times when you quietly hang up the phone, hold your head in your hands for a few minutes, and wonder if you're on a treadmill that is moving faster than you can run.

After hanging up the phone, I called Rosie back in my office and said, "I want you to continue to work in the office, and we will still work on the profanity. Will that be okay?"

She gave me one of those sweet broad toothy smiles and said, "Thank you," and headed to class.

The Numbers Racket

As mentioned previously, Rosie continued working in the office trying to improve her vocabulary and reduce her use of four-letter words. She was making improvement, but not by leaps and strides. She was beginning to have a few profanity-free conversations.

With eight hundred students in my particular section of the school, we made it a policy for students not to use the office phone. This was in order to keep the phone lines open in case a parent needed to contact us, which happened frequently. There were eight pay phones in the school, and we asked the students to use them. Most students complied with our request, but a few made a habit of using the office phone, especially if the secretary was out of the office.

One of these individuals was Rosie. Mrs. Joyce Robinson, my secretary, didn't hold Rosie strictly to the rules because she worked in the office, was sweet, and we were trying to improve her conversation abilities. I was in the office when Rosie came by and made a phone call at 11:00 a.m. just before her lunch. She used the phone about the same time each day.

I asked my secretary, "Do you know why Rosie is using the phone each day around lunchtime?" I was wondering if her mother might be ill, and they had a prearranged time for Rosie to check on her."

Mrs. Robinson said, "I am not aware of any problems or illness, but Rosie does come by daily to use the phone about the same time. I haven't stopped her because she is on the phone for maybe ten to fifteen seconds."

Most of the time, Rosie would tell the person she was talking with, "Thank you," hang up, and go about her business. Occasionally,

Rosie would slap her hands together and say "All right" after hanging up the phone and then skip away from the office.

The next week, I stood across from the office at the time Rosie usually made her phone call and watched the scene unfold.

Rosie walked into the office, picked up the phone, dialed her number, and said, "This is Rosie," waited for about five or ten seconds and said, "Thank you," hung up the phone, and went on her way.

This happened four out of five days that week. During the week, I asked Rosie if anyone was sick or if there were any problems at home.

She would flash her beautiful smile and say, "Everybody's fine."

This was a mystery to me. I talked to other administrators and teachers, and no one had any idea what a five- to ten-second phone call could mean. I did not want to call Rosie into the office and ask her about the phone calls because she was doing better eliminating profanity from her conversations, and her grades were improving; calling her into the office might scare her and could possibility cause her to backslide. I asked Mrs. Robinson if she could to find out what Rosie was doing on the phone. Rosie came by while I was talking to Mrs. Robinson.

Rosie picked up the phone, dialed a number, listened for a few seconds, and then said, "Thank you," and hung up.

Mrs. Robinson said, "Wait a minute, Rosie. I need your help sorting these papers if you have a few minutes."

Rosie went into the workroom with Mrs. Robinson and began sorting the papers. After a few minutes, my secretary asked, "What are you doing on the phone every day?"

Rosie looked up and said with a big grin and a little blush, "I was calling about my numbers."

Mrs. Robinson had no idea what she was talking about.

"What numbers?"

"Oh, you know, the numbers. I call each day to see if I won."

"What are you talking about, Rosie?"

Rosie was excited to explain the numbers game. She said, "Each day, I put a dime on a set of numbers. If I guess the numbers right,

I will win some money. The more numbers I guess right, the more money I get."

It was much like the present-day lottery system, but at this time, the numbers racket was illegal.

"If I win, I go by the house on the way home and pick up my money in a brown paper bag."

"Do you ever win?"

Rosie replied "Sometimes."

We ask Rosie not to use our phone to check her numbers, and she was perfectly okay with not calling.

She said, "I will just go by and check my numbers after I get off the school bus."

Mrs. Robinson did an excellent job in handling the situation. I could always depend on her. That ended our involvement with the South Nashville numbers racket, and thankfully, no one was the wiser.

Early Training Could Be Hazardous to Your Health

Being raised in the 1950s, children learned to do as they were told without any replies such as "Why?" "What?" "That does not make sense," or "I won't do it." Very few questioned the adults. If one did question, the answer was, "Because I said so" with a stern look and a possible warp on the rear. I am not sure why this was the prevailing attitude of the time. Maybe it was the way it had always been.

One societal change that may have contributed to this attitude was World War II. Many of the adults during this time had served in the armed forces and were taught to obey orders; following orders could be the difference between life and death. I feel there was some carryover from the war that helped develop the "do as I say" attitude. Being on the receiving end of that attitude helped form the basis for my actions during my early adult life.

With that background, I progressed to the turbulent 1970s when attitudes were changing rapidly on a personal, as well as the social, basis. During this time, I was a small school principal at McGavock High. The building had thirteen and one-half acres under one roof and was originally planned to combine two schools: Two Rivers and Donelson High, which were intense rivals. The federal court entered the mix and ruled that Cameron High, a successful black school, was to be closed and its students sent to McGavock.

No one was happy about the situation. At times, disgruntled students would attempt to retaliate. One of the major retaliatory methods was *bomb scares.*

Technology was in its infancy, and there were no cell phones or anyway to easily trace a call. One of the emerging pranks was to call and say a bomb had been placed in the school and quickly hang up the phone. The school policy was to evacuate the school when there was a bomb threat. The students and teachers were told we were having a fire drill to reduce confusion and possible panic.

One of these prank callers was kind enough to give us a time and area of the impending explosion. The explosive device was supposedly placed in one of the thousand student lockers.

The executive principal called the four small school principals and said, "We have received a bomb threat, and it is in one of the student lockers. There is enough time for a search. Check each locker and see if you can locate the bomb and do not tell anyone why you are searching the lockers."

I retrieved the special locker key and moved toward the lockers. The students were required to use combination locks that could be opened with this special key. It allowed for searches in situations such as this.

A small voice in my head came forward with the statement, "Are you nuts? If you find a bomb, what are you going to do? It might explode."

My childhood training of "do as you are told" won over the logic of my internal voice, and I began the search. In the first several lockers, I found nothing but books, trash, decaying food, coke cans, and two lacy bras, one black and one red. Finding bras in lockers was not too unusual as the 1970s was the emerging of the women's liberation movement. The way for women to show support for this movement was to go braless. The female students would leave home with bras in place, and when they arrived at school, the bras would come off and go into their lockers. These actions sometimes caused other disruptive problems.

I continued to open lockers, and near the end of my search, I found one that had a piece of wood wedged at the top of the door. When I removed the wood, the door sprung sideways and jammed. I steadily tugged on the door, and it partially opened with a loud metallic scraping rattle that caused me to flinch. Straining, I pulled the door open just enough to peer inside. What I saw was cause for more apprehension.

Inside the paper-trashed locker, I could faintly see what appeared to be two black wires protruding from the left bottom corner. I began carefully prying the door open and put my hand inside. After slowly pulling crumpled paper and a coke can away from the left bottom of the locker, I could plainly see two black wires emerging from behind the last remaining piece of paper. As I carefully removed the paper, I froze. What I saw almost made me need fresh pants.

Crammed in the corner of the locker was a bluish-green blob with two wires rising from behind it. Having watched television programs such as *Mission Impossible*, I knew the dangers and description of C-4 plastic explosives.

The little voice appeared again, asking this simple question, "What in the hell are you doing here?"

I paid no attention to this intelligent voice, again revealing my stupidity. In the few seconds of this discovery, I also noticed two brownish-black projections emanating from the bottom of the green blob. Was this the ignition device? Where was the timer and, more importantly, how much time did I have before the bomb exploded?

This revaluation made me examine the light-green C-4 explosive more closely. Located in the center of the green blob was a dark crease-like indention with faded illegible print on each side. By this time, my heartbeat had increased, hands were shaking, and sweat was trickling from under my arms and down my brow, as well as other places.

At first glance, I assumed the dark indention was a crease where two bricks of plastic explosives had been pressed together. The crease was where the ignition cap was generally placed. That was the exact place I saw two brownish-black projections emerging from the green blob. My little voice did not say a word. I think he had left the building.

My little but now much louder head voice reappeared to rescue me and said, "Fool, get out of here and take your office staff with you."

I had not moved during this entire visual examination, which took only seconds but seemed like hours. After I regained my composure, I cautiously, and with great effort, pried opened the warped locker door a few more inches. The additional light allowed a better examination of the C-4 explosives. The light also revealed the true origin of the perceived danger.

I had discovered crammed in the left corner of the locker, a light-greenish-blue mold covering an old Big Mac hamburger. The black wires consisted of a bent coat hanger lodged behind the hamburger. The brownish-black ignition caps were old french fries.

I stopped my search and slowly walked back into my office, sat down behind my desk, had a nervous chuckle, checked my pants, and told no one about my *Mission Impossible* plastic explosives.

Changing Your Color

Suddenly merging two different societies can often overwhelm some individuals. Rather than continuing to fight and try to understand and blend with this new society, they quit. It's easier to quit, especially if blame of failure can be placed on someone else. There were several students, both black and white, that fell into this category. In my opinion, it was our job to try to help these particular individuals bridge this social gap.

Ronald Harris, from his records, appeared to be of average intelligence and one that could succeed if he put effort into his academic work. He was much like the majority of the students that attend school—they could if only they would. Ronald had absolutely quit; he did not do his work, did not attend class, and the only thing that he was consistent in was showing up for lunch. For the remainder of the time, he would find a place to hide in this mammoth school.

After trying several things to encourage him, I was left no alternative but to call his mother again and, this time, demand she come in for a parent conference. I did not like requiring this of the black community due to the financial hardship that it placed on them. A large portion of the black parents resided in public housing and did not own a car. That required them to get a friend or take a taxi to school, which was well over ten miles from their home.

In Ronald's case, I had no alternative. I had tried every trick in the book, and none had any effect on his behavior.

Her first reply was "I will talk to Ronald and get him to do better."

"Mrs. Harris, we have already tried that twice, and we got no change in Ronald. No, you are going to have to come to school. You, Ronald, and I are going get this problem corrected, one way or another."

She pleaded, "I don't have a way to get to school."

"Mrs. Harris, I know this will be difficult, but we are doing this because of Ronald's behavior. He is doing absolutely nothing, and this attitude has to change. Find a way to school and keep Ronald home with you until you do. You can ride the school bus if you like. I will make the arrangements."

She finally agreed to come to the school, and a date was set for our conference.

The day I was to meet with Ronald and his mother did not start well. It was as cold as a polar bear's rear, and I broke my window scraper on the thick coat of frost spread across the windshield. The old Volkswagen camper I was driving, having an air-cooled engine, did not function well until it was thoroughly warmed up, and that was usually about three quarters the way to work. About a half mile from the school, I heard a "pow" and rumble that shook the back of the camper. My first thought was the engine had blown up as it had done once before. Luck was with me this time; it was a flat tire. I got my jack and spare tire while mumbling dirty words to myself. Just as I was getting ready to dirty my hands on the tire, some students driving by took pity on me and stopped to help.

The driver said, "Dr. Hargis, stand over there, and we will have this done in just a minute."

All these young men were auto mechanics students, and they worked as efficiently as a NASCAR pit crew.

When we got to school, my rescuing students went to the cafeteria for a doughnuts-milk breakfast, which was their routine. It was my treat this time. After the leisurely breakfast, they were late for their first-period class.

The spokesperson of the group came into my office and sheepishly said, "Dr. Hargis, we are late for class. Can you help us?"

I said, "You need a note for class?"

The young men had been very helpful. I was glad to write them the excuse for their five-minute tardy. Maybe this was their first lesson in politics, or maybe not.

Along with the two parent conferences scheduled that day, I had fifteen student discipline referrals from teachers. Mrs. Robinson sent for the referred students, and I worked with them until time for my first parent conference. This conference was with white parents whose son had been suspended for fighting. Normally, the penalty for fighting was both individuals involved in the fight were suspended no matter who threw the first punch unless there were extenuating circumstances. In this particular situation, their son, William, not only started the fight but also inflicted injuries that required medical attention. The parents came in and sat down without saying a word.

They were already angry because of missing work. Then they suddenly blurted out, "Our son would only fight if someone started it, and that nigger was sitting in his seat and would not get up."

They were on the attack before I had said one word.

I explained, "There are no assigned seats in the cafeteria. The young man that your son fought was sitting there before William got to the table. I talked to witnesses who saw the fight."

The parents' rapid response was, "That ain't so."

I said, "Yes, it is."

The situation was becoming heated, so I wanted to terminate the conference as soon as possible.

The mother said, "Can William come back to school tomorrow?"

"No, William has a five-day suspension and may return to school in five days."

"What about that nigger? When's he coming back?" shouted the father.

My stern response was "Tomorrow if the swelling goes down around his eyes and he can see."

"This ain't fair. I'm going to the board of education" was the response.

Before I could offer the board of education's phone number, they jumped up, jerked the door open, and walked out, stopping only long enough to turn and call me "A nigger-loving son of a bitch."

I had been called that before. I was glad to see them go.

Ronald and his mother were waiting in the outer office. Unfortunately, they observed William's parents leaving and heard them call me a "*nigger-loving son of a bitch*." I don't think that comment impressed Mrs. Harris one way or another. I asked Mrs. Harris and Ronald to come into my office. I could tell by the expression on her face that this was going to be another unpleasant conference.

The first thing out of Mrs. Harris's mouth after I asked her to have a seat was "You are picking on Ronald 'cause he's black. That's the way you damn honkies are."

The day had not been good, and it appeared to be getting worse. Mrs. Harris had just stepped on my last nerve attacking me before I had said one word.

Without hesitating or thinking, I said, "Mrs. Harris, if being black is causing Ronald to behave the way he has, then maybe we should try to see if there's a way to change his color."

Boy, did that statement escalate the animosity in the room. It was like pouring gas on a fire. Mrs. Harris stood, waving her hands and shouting obscenities that I could barely understand and some I had never heard before.

When she stopped to get her breath, I said, "Are you through yelling?"

She glared at me and said nothing. I took the opportunity to say, "We are both here for the same reason, and that is to help Ronald."

After I made the second statement, she did calm down enough for us to have a limited conservation. We talked about Ronald's situation and him not attending class. Ronald did not say a word. The interesting thing that I noticed about Ronald was that when I made the statement about changing his color, Ronald did not get mad, he just hung his head.

After a short discussion, Mrs. Harris and I got a commitment from Ronald that he would do better. As we were leaving the office, it was time for lunch, and Ronald wanted to know if he could stay at school.

"If you will go to class and do what we agreed, then yes, you can stay. I'll write you a note to get into class."

Ronald went straight to the cafeteria. His never missing a lunch even when skipping class made me wonder if he was receiving the proper amount of food at home.

I turned to Mrs. Harris and said, "Goodbye, Mrs. Harris. Thank you for coming."

She left without saying a word. I hoped she left with a better attitude toward the school.

In less than one day, I had been called a "nigger-loving son of a bitch," a "black-hating honky," and other names I could not understand. It had been less than a grand day.

William did not learn from his experience. I saw him in my office several times after the parent conference.

Ronald was a different story. He was never sent to my office again after the parent conference. He went to class, made decent grades, and graduated. I've often wondered where life's road took each of them.

A Short Event

A school with three thousand students, one hundred thirty-five teachers, and a physical plant of thirteen acres under one roof causes simple communication sometimes complex. To alleviate this problem, the administrative staff met each Thursday to plan the next week's agenda. We as principals of the small schools would impart this schedule to the teachers at a faculty meeting the following Monday. If an administrator was late for one of these meeting, it usually meant that he was dealing with a problem. About midway through one of these meetings, the absent administrator entered the room with a solemn face. No one asked him why he was late, and he did not volunteer any information. Later that day, information started creeping through the gossip grapevine.

The night before or early that morning, someone entered the principal's office and left a gift for him. When he entered his office that morning, on his desk was a perfectly placed dinner setting. This consisted of a cafeteria plate and eating utensils arranged for a formal banquet. The main course was lying in the middle of the plate.

According to the gossip, the main course in the center of the plate was an eight-inch-long brown "turd," slightly tapered on one end and blunt on the other. The morsel was laid curving perfectly with the edge of the plate and with a generous sprinkling of parsley. Someone was well acquainted with proper dinning etiquette. It was rumored that the main course appeared to be of human origin.

I don't think the person responsible for this meal was ever apprehended and given his proper reward. Even if you caught this rogue chef, how would you write the discipline report that would be sent to the district office? Sometime you have to scrape things off life's plate and move forward.

FOREVER IN CHRISTMAS

Christmas is supposed to be a time of joy and happiness. Most everyone is in a jovial mood. Generally, the students' emotions are two clicks above normal. I never enjoyed Christmas until school was out for the now-called "winter holidays." The name was changed so that no one would be offended; this is known as being "politically correct."

Prior to political correctness, the two weeks of vacation during December was simply called Christmas vacation. No one was bent out of shape because their religious belief was not publicly recognized. A person's religion or belief was personal, and it was treated that way. Today everyone wants his or her orthodoxy ten minutes in the sun.

Another problem this time of the year was exams. There were years when midterm examinations were given before Christmas holidays—oh, excuse me, "winter vacation." Other years, they were after Christmas. Tests, no matter when they were given, added stress for some students and could interfere with their enjoying the holidays.

This was also a time when you could see the vast difference between the haves and the have-nots. Some students would give gifts to teachers and friends at school prior to the holidays. Yesteryear, when the schools were more homogeneous in their makeup, classes would draw names and exchange presents at a party on the last day of school prior to the two-week vacation. Even with neighborhood schools, there were some students who found it financially difficult to purchase a gift.

One case in point, which seems a hundred years ago, was during my fifth-grade experience. That event is etched in my mind as if it were yesterday. Everyone had drawn names for the Christmas party. When all the presents were given out, I received a small cylindrical package wrapped in brown paper cut from a grocery bag. A shoelace was tied in a bow for a ribbon. It looked as if it were a fat first-grade pencil. Everyone was opening their packages, and the room echoed with squeals of "Thank you! Thank you! Thank you!" The name on my package was from a boy of the lower socioeconomic level of our small town. As I untied the shoestring and unrolled the paper, sure enough, it was a writing instrument, a ballpoint pen. When I attempted to use it, the lever that made the ink pen functional was broken.

I knew the individual who gave it to me felt badly because he came to me and said, "If the pen doesn't work, you can take it back to Franklin's Five and Ten Cent store and get another one. That is where I bought it."

I said, "No, it's working fine. Thank you for the pen."

He went back to his seat, surely knowing I had lied. I had mixed emotions about this particular situation and have remembered it all these years. I guess my first emotion was knowing I did not get a gift that equaled the one that I had given. After that initial reaction, I thought about the student that gave me the gift and his feelings. I still remember his name, where he sat in class, and my first personal introduction to inequality. I also remember the pen was blue with a black plunger top bent slightly to the left and nonfunctional.

Today schools have restrictions on parties and giving of gifts, yet the process continues. Many students exchange gifts at school because they will not see their friends during the holidays. These exchanges usually take place in public less supervised areas, such as the cafeteria, between classes, and before and after school. A few presents are always stolen every Christmas. Principals and teachers try to find the thief, but by the time a suspect is found, the item would have disappeared, usually sold, or given away. Very seldom was it ever retrieved.

Another situation that is burned into my memory is of a sophomore football player. He was about five feet eight inches, small waist, and had the chiseled physique of a weight lifter. He was very fast, and the football coach had great aspirations for him in the coming years. Robert wanted to earn money to buy his mother a Christmas present. It was a Monday one week before the holidays. He came to me during lunch and wanted to talk with me for a few minutes.

I asked him into the office and said, "Okay, Robert, what's on your mind?"

He said, "Can you help me find a job so I can earn some money to get Mother a Christmas present?"

I said, "I will see what I can do."

It was four days until the holidays. If I were successful in getting him a job, he would have nine days to work before Christmas. Time was of the essence. I knew the park department had temporary jobs during the holidays in the area where Robert lived. I called the Nashville Park Department. The director was not in his office. I explained my problem to his secretary and asked if she would have him to contact me as soon as possible. Time was slipping by, and I began to think I would be making Robert a loan. The last day before vacation, the park director returned my call. His call was too late as Robert had decided to take matters into his own hands.

I was in my office when the news came that the school cafeteria had been robbed. The lunchroom manager, after everyone had been fed, always took the daily receipts to her office. This was a common procedure, and everyone knew she was counting the money.

The police arrived and began to interview the cafeteria director. They asked, "Do you know who robbed you?"

She replied, "The young man walked into my office and said, 'This is a holdup.'" He then pulled his mask over his face just like they did in the old west days."

"You got a good look at his face?"

"Yes, he is a football player."

"Is there anything else you can tell us about this person?"

"I think they call him Turbo," she replied. Turbo was Robert's street name.

The police and administrators began looking for Robert, not really expecting to find him at school. As the police left the cafeteria office, Robert rounded the corner by the gymnasium. The police shoved Robert against the wall and handcuffed him.

Robert looked around, wide-eyed and fearful, shouting, "What did I do? What did I do?"

The police took Robert downtown and booked him for armed robbery.

I was told a few weeks later that he had planned the robbery even before he had come to me seeking work. His plan had consisted of robbing the cafeteria, taking the money to the football field, and hiding it in a trash can. Robert had put extra clothes in the trash container earlier that morning. After putting the money in the trash can, he changed clothes and came back to the school. His thought process was that no one would recognize him as the robber because of his mask and wearing another set of clothes. His mistake was announcing it was a holdup and then pulling his mask over his face. The cafeteria manger recognized him immediately when the police brought him to her for identification.

The park director called me a few days later. I told him that we did not need his help; the situation had taken care of itself. I never told him what really happened. I saw no need to burden him with the developments that had occurred. I felt bad enough for both of us.

Robert was suspended from school for the remainder of the year. Being a juvenile, he was released from jail in his mother's custody. He was free until his court appearance. There must have been a backlog of cases as his court date was late summer. Unfortunately, he never had his day in court. At the beginning of the following school year, I learned that in midsummer, Robert decided to take over the drug trafficking in his community. This was a big mistake. On a hot July night, he was approached by another drug dealer and was shot close range in the face and chest with a double barrel twelve-gauge shotgun. He had no chance of surviving.

Not a Christmas goes by that I do not think of Robert and this terrible situation. I will always wonder if a job would have resulted in a different outcome.

HEATHER AND THE GOVERNOR

In 1971, McGavock High School was not only the newest school in the state, but it was also the largest, which attracted attention. The new governor, like most politicians, always look for interesting and positive places to visit for publicity purposes. McGavock High School fit that bill perfectly.

We were informed a week in advance that he would be visiting our campus. The staff and students were told, hoping everyone would be on their best behavior. The day of the visit the school was spotless, and for the most part, there were no students in the halls during classes.

I was a proud new father, and my wife asked about bringing our daughter to school and showing her off.

When she suggested that, I quickly replied, "Sure, bring her."

That morning while getting dressed in my best going-to-church suit, I turned to my wife and said, "I forgot. This is the day the governor is coming to school."

My wife asked, "Do you want to cancel bringing Heather to school?"

"Yeah, you had better not come today."

After a short pause, I said, "The governor will not be there until ten o'clock. Can you be there at nine o'clock? You can be in and out of the school before the politicians get there."

Right on time, my wife came in with my beautiful daughter. She gave Heather to me, and I began showing her to everyone. I completely forgot about the governor, and so did my daughter. I had her lying on my shoulder. As I moved through the admiring group, I gave Heather a few love pats on the back. *Big mistake!*

Those love pats signaled to Heather it was time to release the gas and undigested food that had been lingering in her upper digestive system. Heather responded with "Wolop, wolop." She always did everything to her maximum such as the time we were in the car going to a party. She released a projectile vomit stream from the back seat of the car to the front windshield. I never did get everything cleaned out of the defroster vents.

I looked down at her and my best Sunday suit. Once again, she did her best. Heather began to whimper as my wife took her. We were watching a slowly pulsating, oozing glob of white pabulum soak into the right lapel of my suit. It was 9:45 a.m., the governor was at the school, waiting for the media to set up. *What to do? What to do?* raced through my mind.

Mrs. Robertson, my secretary, took charge and, with a wet cloth, began to wipe the goo. It did not wipe. The wiping spread the now ill-smelling goo off my lapel onto my jacket pocket just below my snazzy handkerchief. She looked up and said, "This is not going to work."

The central office secretary called and said, "Dr. Hargis needs to get over here if he is going to get in the picture, and Mr. Lafever wants everyone over here pronto."

We made one last desperate attempt to clean the entrenched, clump of Heather's ill-smelling goo from my jacket. It failed. The only thing to do was dump the coat and head to the photo shoot in shirtsleeves. I made the deadline. Somewhere under a pile of dusty old papers, there is a photo of the governor with a group of sharply dressed gentlemen, less one in shirtsleeves.

THE BOMB SCARE

The information concerning the bomb was immediately passed to the person in charge for a decision. Generally, the decision was to vacate the building. Law enforcement research found that persons who make bomb threats usually remained in the general vicinity to watch the fruits of their labor. There was no specific time or method to these pranks. Our job as school officials was to vacate the building as quickly as possible. Getting students to go outside during lunch was sometimes difficult because their food would be cold when they returned. Leaving the building at this time left an irritating foul taste in everyone's mouth for the remainder of the day. (No pun intended.)

As administrators, we ensured that all students and teachers left the building. Then if time permitted, a search for the explosive would be conducted. I often wondered about my sanity when performing that part of my job. There were several bomb scares a year, and generally, we did not apprehend the caller. At this time, the technology was limited for tracing calls. On one occasion, we discovered who made the call. This threat had an interesting twist. I was monitoring the cafeteria, watching students cram down french fries, tartar sauce, and fish sticks.

A student office worker motioned for me to come to her. I could tell by her face that this was not going to be a pleasant conversation.

The student said, "You are needed in the office. Hurry."

When I entered the door, Mrs. Robinson said, "A bomb scare has been called in, and the building is to be evacuated."

Standard operating procedure was not to announce there was a bomb in the building. All administrators were alerted concerning the situation, and the evacuation was called a fire drill. Each school was required to have one fire drill a month by state law. During the 1970s, we had no problem making that quota. Just as I returned to the cafeteria, the fire bell rang.

Everyone knew it was the fire bell by its distinctive sound. Most assumed it was just a practice fire drill, and nothing to be alarmed about. Many of the students grabbed their fish sticks and a handful of french fries and headed out the door while others took the entire plate with them. There would always be two or three tables where the students continued casually eating. Those were the students that we had to almost force outside. There was griping and complaining, but finally, they would go.

After checking the halls, school personnel would go outside and wait for the all-clear bell to ring so everyone could return to the building. Sometimes students would be outside thirty minutes or more. This always caused scheduling problems. Class adjustments were made for the time missed. Everyone was always irritated about a bomb scare, even the students, especially those eating.

When students become irritated about something and want to see justice served, the name of the culprit will usually come to the surface. Forced to eat cold french fries creates enough anger and displeasure for a person to turn in the guilty culprit. Several students gave a name to us. The student was not under my supervision, so I did not conduct the investigation. I did know the young man and knew that he was a special education student.

The administrator that did the investigation came to my office early the next morning before school started. We discussed the situation over a cup of coffee.

He said, "The student readily admitted making the call. He gave me all the details, which pay phone he used, and where he got the money to make the call. This was the interesting part. He borrowed a dime from Mrs. McGee, his guidance counselor."

This particular guidance counselor, Mrs. Rob McGee, was as good as gold and always tried to help students. She was a mainstay in the functioning of the entire school.

She received a lot teasing for a month or so with people playfully badinaging her about furnishing money for the bomb scare. Even today forty-five years later, if I saw her, I would smile and chuckle a little, and she would know exactly what I was thinking. She was a dedicated educator whom I greatly respected.

McGavock's Intramural Program

McGavock High School, with all its pluses, such as an extensive curriculum and a physical plant that was beyond anything in the state of Tennessee, had one major flaw: reduced athletic opportunities for many students.

As the McGavock athletic director, I was concerned that there were students with athletic ability not going out for sports because they thought they did not have a chance to make the team.

When three high schools are combined into one, the reduction ratio is three to one. An example is the basketball team, which normally has fifteen members on a squad. Before the consolidation, forty-five student athletes had the privilege of participating. The reduction of thirty students not having this opportunity weighed heavily on me. It was not good educational policy. Any administrator will tell you that a good athletic program has a tremendously positive influence on the atmosphere of the school. This produces a better learning environment, which is the ultimate school goal.

McGavock's organization had students divided into small schools; each division had approximately seven hundred fifty students with one principal. The four individual schools would lend itself to having four athletic teams. If this had been allowed, the increase would have been three teams to four. The increase of one team would allow fifteen more students to participate in basketball. This team increase for every sport would have been a major positive impact for the school.

Unfortunately, this was not to be. This travesty lays at the feet of the Tennessee Secondary School Athletic Association (TSSAA), which governs all the athletic programs in the state of Tennessee. The executive principal of McGavock, Mr. Chester Lafever, partitioned the TSSAA to allow McGavock to have a team for each small school. His request was denied by the TSSAA. This decision was based on the TSSAA bylaws, which states that only one team is allowed for each school. The word school was interpreted as one building according to the information I received.

Having four teams would have been very difficult to implement and very expensive. The Metropolitan Nashville school board did not pay any cost of athletic programs. Even when taking into account the problems of scheduling and expense, I personally felt that it would have been a positive improvement and would have eliminated many adverse situations that developed.

During my second year as an administrator, I talked with the executive principal on numerous occasions about developing an intramural program. He acknowledged that this program was needed but was afraid this might increase racial tension. This was a valid concern. In fact, there were a few times that the school had to undergo lockdowns to reduce the possibility of widespread violence. His concern was justified, but without an opportunity for the release of tension, it was only a matter of time until increased violence could develop.

Each week, there was an administrative meeting to plan for next week's activities. This consisted of the four small school principals, the curriculum coordinator, and the executive principal. At least once a month, I would bring up the lack of an intramural program during these meetings.

After several weeks of bringing up the subject, the executive principal turned and glared at me and said, "Okay, Hargis, do your intramural program, but I'm telling you, it had better work!"

I replied, "That is all I wanted to hear."

The first thing in organizing the intramural program was to develop a list of activities that would be made available to the students. Some of these activities would be self-organized and implemented by the students themselves, such as bridge, chess, checkers, and other board and card games. Other activities offered were the following: arm wrestling, tug-of-war, free throw shooting, and of course, everyone's favorite, basketball. To get this program organized and implemented was going to take cooperation of the McGavock staff.

One of the major concerns was to make sure that all teams were properly integrated. That means having an equal amount of black and white students on each team when possible. Having an all-black or all-white team would increase the tension within the school. It was suggested that dividing the students interested in the programs by alphabet would solve that problem. After a quick survey and a preliminary test, it was determined that this plan resulted in racially diverse teams.

The next problem was obtaining help. Cooperation from the physical education (PE) department would be imperative. Head of the PE department, Omega Stratton, was excited about the program and agreed to help implement it. We discussed areas that were critical to the success of the program with PE instructors, Doris Rogers, Tilly Crockett, and Bill Randolph. All agreed, three major areas of concern were the following: adult coaches for the basketball teams, officials to call the games, and most importantly, safety.

The basketball teams would require adult coaches. If we could not get teacher cooperation, this segment of the program would be dropped. At the next faculty meeting, teachers were given the opportunity to coach a team, and we had a very positive response. The McGavock faculty, for the most part, were dedicated educators and would go well beyond normal hours to help students and without additional pay.

The basketball officials were members of the varsity basketball team. This gave the diversity we needed in officiating and would alleviate any favoritism. They did an outstanding job.

Having everything organized and ready to go, the program was explained at an administrative meeting. The implementation schedules were distributed to the principals. There were two items in the program that met with resistance.

One was the expenditure for small trophies. I wanted to give a trophy to all champions in every sport and activity. There was a basic price and a charge for each letter that was engraved. Giving each participant on championship teams an award would cost several hundred dollars. I countered this resistance by explaining that I had a friend, Marc Horton, and his wife, Esther, who owned Horton's Trophy business. They agreed to give us a wholesale price, which would make the cost reasonable.

The next concern was not so easily solved and could curtail the entire program. The schedule called for the finals to be presented as an assemble program for the entire school. One of the concerns, which I understood, was that fights and other violent encounters usually occur when there are large groups of loosely supervised students. There was no way to eliminate that concern. To counter the possibility, we asked the teachers to bring their homeroom students to the gymnasium and sit with them during the ball games.

Also, police were asked to attend the assembly. The police department had a division called "Youth Guidance" that was dedicated to working with the schools. They moved from school to school as needed. During the games, two officers were to be in attendance.

There was another factor in my plan that I did not discuss with the staff, human nature. Generally, there will not be violent behavior when individuals are satisfying a basic biological need. In this case, the need is enjoyment, humor, and release of pent-up energy. The odds were in favor of a positive outcome as there was nothing at stake, except class bragging rights, small trophies, and an enjoyable time.

After a long discussion and a thorough examination of all aspects of the program, a reluctant approval was given a few minutes after I jokingly reminded the executive principal of his statement, "You can do this, but you better make it work."

I explained, "This program has been organized with every possible safeguard in place. These students deserve an intramural program."

He repeated, "It had better work."

After the administrative meeting, an announcement was made to the students. Each small school office had a sign-up sheet for ever activity. We explained the times for joining would only be before school, at lunch, or between classes. Much to my surprise, we had lines of students waiting to enroll.

The interesting thing was that students enlisted to participate in many of the nontraditional programs, such as chess, checkers, bridge, and arm wrestling. We had a few students that wanted to extend the program to bowling. I met with them and explained that we could not cover any of the expenses. They agreed to pay the bowling cost. Another sport was added to our program.

A deadline was imposed on registration for the programs. No student requested late enrollment. This told me there was high interest from the students. After the deadline, all names were collected and alphabetized for team division.

The team's rosters were developed, and brackets were designed. Activities, such as board and card games, were conducted on an individual basis. The students would look at the brackets for the name of their opponent. With the help of the school secretaries, they would find their contestant and schedule a time and place for their game. Many times, this was a student they were not acquainted with, which aided school socialization. The winner would report the results to my office, and their name would be moved forward on the tournament bracket. This process would continue until a champion was determined.

The students that were interested in arm wrestling were called to my office to compete. Over twenty male students signed up for arm wrestling. Even though they had the opportunity, no females chose to compete. When the contestants came into my interoffice, the door was closed, and the students were given instructions. When they assumed the position on the carpeted floor, the count was one, two, three, go. During the contest, there were a lot of moans, groans, and grunts coming from behind the door. I often wondered what other students who were not aware of activities thought when they came into the office. I never had any comments, but my secretary told me that she saw several quizzical looks.

The physical education department had the equipment for the tug-of-war, a long rope two inches in diameter. This contest took place during lunchtime or after school. Both girls and boys had teams. When I went to the gymnasium to observe the tug-of-wars, I always found it interesting that students not involved in the activity got excited and started yelling for the team of their choice. After the competition was over, everyone seemed to be in a jovial mood, and the opponents were laughing and talking with one another. It was good to see interracial activity with a smile on the face.

We had several basketball teams, and each team had a volunteer coach. There were no rules or regulations regarding practice. Most coaches tried to have one or two organized practices that took place after school and was scheduled through the physical education department. This caused a dilemma for some black participants because most of them lived ten to twelve miles away from school and did not have transportation. Many of the teacher/coaches carried those students' home after practice. Later, I was told that if the coach could not carry the students, their white teammates who had cars would give them a ride.

Most of the teachers took their coaching responsibility seriously and wanted to win. The tournament bracket was organized through classes—sophomore, junior, and senior. All teams in each class played one another in single elimination tournaments. Therefore, there would have be a champion of the sophomore, junior, and senior class. All these games were played after school. The finals of basketball and tug-of-war were scheduled during an assembly before the entire student body. This was the day that our executive principal was concerned about or, should I say, was dreading.

One reason for his concern was the gymnasium capacity was approximately two thousand. McGavock's enrollment was approximately three thousand, which would be a thousand extra students crammed into the gym. There would have been extensive overcrowding. When you considered the students that were absent, those participating and early dismissals, the numbers dropped considerably, but still, this was an overload and could be a volatile situation. I understood his concern, but I was still betting on human nature.

The day for the championship playoffs finally arrived. The announcements shortly before the activity asked for those students who were involved in the championship basketball and tug-of-war to please report to the gymnasium.

After a few minutes, classes were dismissed by homerooms to the gymnasium, seniors first, juniors, and sophomores. Teachers were to sit with their homeroom classes. The girls' tug-of-war was first on the agenda—the sophomores versus the seniors. The announcer emphasized the lowly sophomore class was in competition with the ruling senior class. That comment immediately started a chant, which was prevalent at that time, "SENIORS RULE! SENIORS RULE!" The sophomores responded with a few of their own chants. You could feel the excitement building as the opponents readied themselves for battle.

The midcourt line on the basketball floor was used as the starting point. The team that pulled their opponents across this line would be the winner. Teams looked evenly matched, and each had a good anchor at the end of the rope. Most well-designed tug-of-war teams had a rope-end safeguard that was generally the most robust player. This was the case for both teams. To add an interesting wrinkle to the contest, the participants were required to remove their shoes to prevent damage to the gymnasium floor.

They lined up, the whistle blew, and the contest began. The seniors pulled the sophomores a few feet over the centerline, and then the sophomores retaliated and regained the footage. Students wore ragged clothes in those days, especially bell-bottom pants. They were always too long, dragged the ground, and become frayed. This was the style. The senior anchor was definitely in style with her long-frayed pants. As the sophomores begin a slow, steady attack, the senior anchor dug her heels in to stop their progress. While doing this, her pant leg worked its way under her left foot. Each time she gave an extra hard pull, her left foot bore down on her bell-bottom trouser leg, causing her pants to inch down from her waist. As the competition continued, each pull forced her jeans down another inch from her waist. It became obvious to the entire student body when her bright-red panties began to emerge from under her slacks.

She began to realize what was happening and tried to alleviate the problem. You have never seen a more confused individual. She tried to let go of the rope with one hand and pull up her pants. Each time she attempted to pull them up, the sophomores would gain a couple of feet. What a dilemma! Does she expose all for the love of her teammates and victory, or does vanity win out and she let her teammates down? She wrestled with this problem until her bell-bottoms were pulled halfway down her gluteus maximus, exposing most of her red panties.

The entire student body could see her undies as they laughed, screamed, hollered, and pointed. Finally, a decision had to be made; she released her grip on the rope and pulled up her pants while she watched her entire team being jerked across the finish line. Vanity won out.

The announcer awarded the trophy and said, "The sophomore tug-of-war team defeated the seniors by exposing their weakness."

Once again, the students stood up clapped, shouted, and whistled. This set the tone for the remainder of the program. The boys' tug-of-war took place uneventfully.

The girls' championship basketball game went smoothly. The student body seemed to enjoy the game but without any great excitement. It was now time for the boys' basketball game, which pitted the senior class against the junior class. Just looking at the two squads, you would not think this would be an exciting game because the juniors were physically outmatched. One of the players on the junior squad had a deformed arm. The deformity was enough to keep him from playing on a school-sponsored team, but he was a formidable player in the intramural league.

As the game worked into the second half, the juniors were ahead a few points. The young man with the deformity wanted the ball every time so he could shoot. His playing style became so obvious that his teammates were reluctant to throw him the ball. He was trying to make it a one-man show and was somewhat successful as his team was ahead a few points. During the latter part of the game, he wanted to shoot so badly that he started taking the ball away from his teammates.

The coach would call time-out and talk with the showboat player.

He would say, "Okay, whatever you say, Coach." Then he would return to the game and do the same thing he did before. The coach did not like what was happening but was in a quandary; with the players he had, he could not win the game without his problem player.

The senior's coach was a math teacher by the name of Roy Francis. He was an easygoing steady man that could always be depended on. As the game approached, the final minutes, Roy's team had managed to get within two points of the juniors. The disruptive player continued to alienate his teammates, as well as everyone in the gymnasium. When he got the ball, the students would boo, and everyone, including the junior spectators, began to yell and support the senior squad.

During the last few minutes of the game, the seniors managed a one-point lead, and the crowd began to yell their support. The junior showboat took the ball away from his teammate in backcourt. Showboat dribbled to the right corner of the floor. One point behind and only seconds to go, he shot the potentially winning basket from the deep right corner. The shot arched high and slowly started downward. The ball hit the rim and bounced to the top edge of the backboard. Slowly it fell downward toward the goal. It was so quiet you could hear a pin drop. The ball hit the front of the goal, balanced there for a second, and then fell from the rim. The rebound was muscled away from the juniors by a big senior forward. One quick pass down court, and the horn sounded.

The seniors won by one point. The entire crowd was standing, yelling, and clapping. Everyone could hear above the roar, "SENIORS RULE! SENIORS RULE!"

Trophies were presented, and everyone exited the gymnasium without a problem. There was not a frown on anyone's face. It was over, and both my boss and I were glad.

I may be wrong, but it was my impression that after the intramural activities, race relations improved.

At least in my small school, we had fewer racial conflicts. Intramurals allowed students to get to know and depend on one another in a pleasant nonforced environment. They had to cooperate in team activities to succeed. Another important factor to the success of the program was the willingness of the teachers and students to provide transportation to those who had none.

When coaching, I participated in carrying students home after practice. Each coach would rotate days driving players home. Many times, white players who had automobiles would carry black teammates home. The school athletic department gave students gas money who made several trips to the inner city. After two years, the school acquired a bus to transport students' home from all after-school activities. The automotive department was saddled with maintenance of the old bus. Robert Evans, an automotive instructor, did a remarkable job keeping the yellow dog express moving.

The intramural program was a success. In my opinion, there was less racial tension in the building. I do not remember anyone saying that this activity was positive for the school or they were glad we did it. No one in authority suggested we continue the intramural program the next year.

The following year, several students asked, "Are we going to have intramurals this year?"

My reply was "You will have to talk to the executive principal."

To my knowledge, that's the only time an intramural program was implemented at McGavock High School.

McGavock's Legal Attempted Rape

The day started normally. Students were racing to their classes—some with no books, and others with their backpacks full, causing them to walk like hunchback old men. I'm sure many students with full backpacks were hoping to obtain knowledge through osmosis. At any rate, for academia, seeing the full backpacks was impressive. I tried to be in the hall to monitor the changing of classes. Just being visible had a calming effect on those that were planning disruptive activities.

After the tardy bell, I went to my office to see what had transpired during my absence. As I entered the door, my secretary handed me a stack of discipline referrals. The first thing I look at on a referral is the name of the teacher sending it. Knowing the sender allows me to develop a priority list. Some teachers have less ability to control students than others. Usually, their discipline style results in some type of conflict. There was one teacher that sent over two hundred referrals in one year.

By ten thirty, I had worked halfway through the discipline list. Now it was time to monitor the cafeteria. Having three thousand students with only four small serving lines forced lunch to begin at an early hour. On the surface, eating at ten thirty does not seem reasonable. However, considering that school starts at seven o'clock and most students were pulled out of bed at five o'clock and dashed off to school without breakfast, an early lunch could be viewed positively.

The lunch period was thirty minutes long. They used this time to eat, go to the restroom, or whatever activities they might want to pursue. During lunch, students were loosely monitored as they moved freely in designated areas.

I was monitoring the cafeteria and trying to keep a close eye on those who were attempting to leave their trays on the table. This was a game of cat and mouse between the students and cafeteria monitors. I found it interesting that students would go to McDonald's or Hardee's and always take their trays back, but not so in school. I guess it was their way of pushing back against authority. While gazing over a cafeteria full of kids, sloppy joes, and tater tots, an office worker rushed over, grabbed my arm, and said in a very excited high-pitched voice, "Dr. Hargis, Dr. Hargis, Mr. Currie wants you right now!"

Mr. James Currie was the principal of the North school, which was located across the cafeteria. He was a good-natured, no-nonsense person that I respected very much. I knew if he needed to see me right now, it was serious. I wasted no time getting to his office.

Entering, I saw a student from my school sitting in a corner with Mr. Currie watching him. The top of the secretary's desk was scattered with papers, the telephone on the floor, and the secretary was standing with her arm around a girl who appeared frightened and in a state of confusion. She was breathing hard, red-faced, and her hair going in every direction. I did not know the young lady, but I assumed that she was an office worker.

Mr. Currie, with a disgusted look on his face, said, "Do you know this young man?"

I replied, "Yes, that is Jimmy. What happened?"

Mr. Currie took him by the arm and ushered us into his inter-office. He was in special education and had only been sent to me once—for making inappropriate remarks in a group of mixed company. (Mixed company is referring to male and female. This is long before gender political correctness became our nations focal point.)

Mr. Currie explained that he had become infatuated with the office worker and attacked her by pushing her down on the secretary's desk. Before anyone had time to recover from the shock and react, he was pulling and tearing at her blouse. Realizing what was happening, a couple of students and the secretary pulled the attacking student off her and restrained him. After what had just transpired, I was surprised that Jimmy had such a calm demeanor. He spoke very little and answered questions mostly with hand motions.

When asked why he did this, his answer was a shrug of his shoulders with an open hand motion.

We were getting nowhere, so I said, "I will take him to my office."

As we left Mr. Currie, I took Jimmy by the arm. I was not sure what he might do, maybe run. He made no attempt to run or jerk away. We walked into my office, and I said, "Sit down," and motioned him to the chair located to the side of the desk, so if necessary, I could get to him quickly.

I was not interested in trying to climb over my desk to stop him from running out the door. I was considered young, but not desk-jumping young. After talking with Jimmy for a few minutes, I realized that he was not going to give any satisfactory answers. The only thing to do was start the standardized procedure that the school system had set up for inappropriate action.

I called his parents, informed them what had happened, and explained that Jimmy would be suspended from school, pending a disciplinary hearing. The school system rules were a one- to ten-day suspension. The administrator had the discretion to determine the number of suspension days depending upon the severity of the misconduct. Any action such as possession of drugs, using drugs, or possession of a knife or gun was a mandatory ten-day exclusion from school followed by a disciplinary hearing. The police were called for weapon violations. (Fifteen years later, when I was a member of the school board, a policy was adopted that any student found with a weapon could be removed from school for an entire year.) At this time, the most severe penalty I could give a student was a ten-day suspension, pending a disciplinary hearing.

Jimmy's parents informed me that they couldn't get Jimmy until later in the day. I kept him within arm's distance until they arrived at four o'clock. I explained the situation and told them to keep Jimmy home until they heard from the district office. Neither parent seemed to be overly distraught. Their actions and demeanor seemed to say, *we've been here before.*

The following day, after all the required reports were completed, I informed the district office of the situation and asked, "Is there anything special I need to do considering this particular incident is not the norm?"

The voice on the phone said, "Let me check. I will call you back shortly." Shortly took longer than I expected. It appeared everyone was taking this problem very seriously.

I was told two days later, "No extra reports need to be completed, but just make darn sure that everything is accurately documented."

I had talked with everyone that witnessed the incident, except the victim. I did not feel she needed to go through the anguish of reliving this horrible situation.

The paperwork was completed and presented to the district office. After the information was reviewed, a date was set for Jimmy's hearing—seven days after the incident occurred. I was not sure what the decision of the disciplinary committee would be, but I did know that this young man needed special help.

The members of the discipline board usually consisted of a school psychologist, uninvolved principal, teacher, and the coordinator from the district office. A special education supervisor would attend the meetings if it involved a special education student. Generally, there would be no more than seven or eight people attending. Due to the type of transgression that had occurred, this student would not attend.

I walked into the hearing room and felt there must have been double scheduling. There were at least twelve people the room. I thought, *I must be in the wrong room.* I started to search for familiar faces and saw the discipline coordinator bringing in additional chairs.

Walking over to her, I said, "Has the hearing location been changed?"

She looked at me with a contorted face and said, "No, all of these people are here for this hearing. This one may be a real dilly."

That statement didn't do anything to ease my anxiety.

Finally, when enough chairs and tables were secured for everyone to have a place to prop their elbows and layout reams of paper, the meeting was called to order. As introductions were made, I began to see what the coordinator meant when she had said, "A real dilly." There were four individuals from an organization with the acronym of EACH. These letters stood for "Educational Advocate for Children with Handicaps." Attending was a special education advocate, a psychologist from the EACH organization, and others that I could not identify. The room was crowded, and I could tell we had lawyers in the group by the way they were opening their leather-zippered notebooks and preparing to take notes. My mind was racing, trying to figure out why are so many outsiders at this meeting. I thought, *Do these parents have powerful friends?*

As the meeting progressed, no one from the EACH organization asked a question. No one doubted that this incident occurred or challenged me on the report. The disciplinary coordinator was getting ready to conclude the meeting and allow the committee to recess and discuss recommendations.

An EACH member bluntly said, "Wait a minute, I have some questions."

It was then I realized why the EACH group had not asked any questions. The chairman of the committee had not given them the opportunity. She was trying to conclude the meeting and send everyone on their way. I thought, *Now it is going to hit the fan.* But I did not have any idea what was going to hit the fan. The incident took place, everything was documented, and it seemed to me that all the bases were covered.

The person I thought was an attorney, I found out later, was a want-to-be attorney and was volunteering with EACH. He pointed a bent, previously broken finger at me and then turned to the committee so they could share in his animosity.

He said, "Are you aware that this young man is categorized as a special education student? All special education students have limitations, for which the school system is required to make adjustments. The school system must allow these students to function in the least restrictive educational environment. Are you aware of this student's limitations?"

The special education supervisor, serving on the committee, barked back, "Yes, we are aware of his handicap. He has difficulty associating with the opposite sex."

"Yes, that is correct." Then turning his bony, crooked finger toward me, he said, "It's your responsibility to make the adjustments for his handicap. Are you aware of this?"

I had walked into this meeting irritated. My main concern was to get the hearing over and hopefully get this student the help he needs. Sometimes when I feel this way, I act before I think. I did not answer his question.

I turned and looked at all of them and said, "The parents of the young lady that was attacked are very upset. They want to know the outcome of this meeting. The results will dictate what actions they will take, which may include a lawsuit. The question that the parents are going to ask is, has justice been properly served? If they decide to sue, whom will they sue? Will they be suing you, you, or you? Will they take legal action against you for impeding decisions that would best serve everyone involved? I am not sure why you are here, but I do know the parents of this young girl are very serious, as you would be, if it had happened to your daughter."

The entire room fell silent. No one said a word for what seemed to be several uncomfortable minutes but was actually only a few seconds. The members of the EACH committee looked at one another, searching for an answer.

The coordinator of the discipline committee took this opportunity to say, "Since there are no other questions, this meeting is adjourned. The results and recommendations will be forthcoming within a week."

The crooked bony-fingered wannabe attorney stated emphatically, "We want a copy of the report."

The committee chairman replied quickly, "Any report that you receive will have to come through a request from the parents. This meeting is adjourned."

The recommendations of the committee resulted in the student being enrolled in a special program outside the school system that specialized in working with individuals that have mental, emotional, and sexual handicaps. This decision was apparently satisfactory as no further action was taken.

Thank God for the Nurse

As usual, I rolled out of bed somewhere between four thirty and five o'clock, stumbled into the bathroom, closed the door, and turned the light on, hoping maybe for once I would not wake my wife. I showered, brushed my teeth, and got ready for a new day, praying it would be uneventful. Walking down the hall without the benefit of lights, I felt my way into the kitchen, got a cup of coffee, a power bar, and headed out the door to my automobile, which was a Volkswagen camper. When I cranked the vehicle, it usually woke everyone in the neighborhood because I had replaced the stock forty-horsepower Volkswagen engine with a 110-horsepower Corvair engine, sporting an automatic transmission. The small Volkswagen camper engine box would not allow for a conventional muffler. I had to install a glass pack muffler, which produced a low rumbling sound. Placing my coffee cup in the holder and my power bar in the passenger seat, I started the engine. It was loud but sounded good. The VW slowly eased out of the driveway and headed to school about 5:45 a.m.

School started early due to the integration process that resulted in busing. The school system did not have enough buses for all students to go to school at the normal time; therefore, high schools started early, and elementary schools began late. All high schools started classes at seven o'clock, which is not an ideal time for any educational program. As I drove out of the driveway, the sun was peeping over the horizon. It was early spring, and everything was beginning to green up. Spring made the world look pleasingly fresh. With few cars on the road, I managed to sip my coffee and eat my packaged breakfast on the way to work. The hot coffee was the only thing that kept me warm because as anyone who has ever owned a Volkswagen knows the heating system leaves much to be desired. I was hoping for a good day. It was Friday, and I was planning to go fishing on Saturday.

As I pulled into the McGavock parking lot, there were a few cars already there. Many of the teachers came to school early and left late. Finishing the last sip of coffee, which was cold, I opened the door and headed into the school. I went through the reception area and entered my small eight-by-ten-foot office. On my desk were stacks of state reports that I had not finished the day before and a stack of discipline referrals that were turned in after school on Thursday. My first procedure each morning was to straighten my desk, look at the calendar for the day's events, take a three-by-five-inch card, and make a list of things to accomplish.

I called another early arriving small school principal, Richard Graves, who was located on the opposite side of the building to discuss a student discipline problem. By the time our conversation was completed, buses began to arrive, and students were strolling into the building. I left the office and went to the front of the school to watch students explode from school bus doors. Some students were chatting and smiling, but most were yawning and rubbing their eyes. The student council sold doughnuts and milk each morning to raise money. That is where the majority of the students would go for their breakfast. Students would buy doughnuts, milk, sit at the tables, yawn at one another, and eat breakfast.

The school was so large that students were allowed seven minutes between classes rather than the traditional five minutes. A minute or two after the first bell, we would encourage the students to move toward their classrooms.

Generally, that would promote comments like "I'm not through eating," "Gimme a minute or two more," or "My teacher won't care if I'm late."

Most would cram their doughnuts down, guzzle their milk, and take off to class. Others would pick up their books, grab their milk and doughnuts, and head to class. There was a rule that no eating was allowed in class, but each teacher had their own classroom rules. It would have been very difficult to enforce the no-eating policy in classrooms and would accomplish nothing but making both teachers and students angry. That particular rule was generally ignored. After escorting a few tardy students to class, I went to my office to check discipline referrals and complete state reports.

Entering my office, I got my second cup of coffee and went to my desk. What a surprise! There were no state reports to complete. I had an excellent secretary, Joyce Robinson, she had taken those reports, completed them, and placed them on the desk for my signature. The only thing I had to do was work the discipline reports. Another pleasant surprise, only eight referrals.

My secretary sent for the students that were referred by the teachers. As they came into my office, I would read their discipline report to them and ask if it were accurate. If the student thought the report was not accurate or there was some inconsistency, I would give them an opportunity to explain their version. After we discussed the situation and if they were determined guilty, they would choose their penalty. I would write the disposition of the case on the referral and return it to the teacher. Guilty students were usually given four choices depending on the severity of the infraction: stay after school for an hour or write some type of research assignment on a subject relating to the infraction or a subject in which they might have an interest. (I never had students write things such as "I will be good" a hundred times. There was no benefit to this type of discipline.) Calling the parents was a choice that most students did not choose. If they had a fear of their parents being contacted, this was used as leverage by telling them if they were sent back with another discipline report, the parents would be called. The last choice was three swats with a paddle. (I've often wondered how many students that were paddled and never returned to the office for a disciplinary problem. I am not aware of any statistical research on this subject. It is thought by many that paddling is a barbaric way of encouraging students to see the light and correct their ways. The counterpoint is that even Mother Nature uses pain to tell you that something is wrong.) Every individual is different, and the more alternatives that are available to encourage them to stay on the right path, the more successful the students and instructors will become.

It was ten o'clock, and with the paperwork completed, it was time to patrol the halls and places that students who were skipping classes might hide. In a building the size of McGavock (thirteen acres under roof), there were plenty of places to hide. Making my rounds, I failed to find anyone in the hall or hiding in any of the crevices. The day was going well, and a smile managed to slip across my face, but I still kept my fingers crossed.

Starting school at seven o'clock in the morning resulted in lunch being served between ten thirty and twelve. School dismissed at two o'clock, so lunch had to be served early to move three thousand students through the lunch line. One of my jobs was to monitor the lunchroom until relief came. It was time for my lunch, which consisted of fish, tater tots, slaw, fruit, and chocolate milk. The lunch tasted good. I am not sure whether it was because I was having a good day, or it was just good food. Both I think. Lunch was over, and it was pushing one o'clock, and all was well.

I asked Mrs. Robinson if anything had happened during lunch. She smiled and said, "No, not yet."

I went into my office, called a friend and colleague, Charles Hailey, the curriculum coordinator, who was located in the center of the building. During our conversation, I told him this was undoubtedly the best day in my educational career, no problems, and just a pleasant workday. The clock moved to five minutes before two, and it was time to monitor students loading the buses. I walked from my desk to the outer office door, and that's when my day dramatically changed.

Standing in the doorway of the office was a young man, about six feet two inches tall, wearing a blood-soaked T-shirt, and blood was streaming down the side of his face.

When our eyes met, he said, "Help me. Please help me."

There was no time to ask what happened as I watched the blood drip from his chin. The bell was going to ring any second, and the halls would be filled with students. Thoughts of what should be done flashed through my mind. I could take him into my inner office and keep him until the students left the building, but that would be twenty minutes or more, and this young man was in serious trouble. Grabbing him by the arm and in a semi-run, I half carried and half drug him to the nurse's office, which was located in the center of the building. Just as we entered the nurse's office, the bell sounded.

The nurse looked up, eyes wide, and said, "Put him on the couch in the back room." She got her medical equipment and said, "Tear his shirt off."

While ripping off his shirt, I noticed eight or ten small puncture wounds in his chest. Oozing from the puncture wounds was frothy red blood making hissing sounds each time he took a breath. The blood was streaming over his chest, puddling on his stomach, and running onto the tan-colored vinyl couch. The nurse was checking his vital signs and listening to his chest with her stethoscope.

She told me in a strained voice, "Put pressure on the chest wound."

Putting my hands over the wounds was not satisfactory as the frothy blood kept bubbling from under my hands. I looked for a bandage. His shirt was on the floor, dirty and soaked with blood. I remembered seeing a towel on the nurse's desk in her outer office. I quickly retrieved the towel and used it to put pressure on the bloody holes in his chest. The hissing sound from his blood-frothing wounds ceased when pressure was applied with the towel.

The nurse was working hard assessing his vital signs, and she kept saying to the student, "Don't leave me. Hang on. Don't leave me!"

Somehow in all the commotion, she had managed to call an ambulance. After his vital signs stabilized, the nurse looked at the wounds on the back and left side of his head. By the time she finished bandaging his head and chest, the ambulance had arrived.

The EMTs put him on a stretcher and, as they rolled the student out of the office, said to the nurse, "You've done a good job."

After the ambulance left, we looked at each other for a moment and then said simultaneously, "Thank you."

As I started out the door, the nurse said, "You better look in the mirror before you leave."

To my surprise, blood was all over my shirt, tie, and the entire right side of my face. I went into the lavatory, got a clean towel, and washed my face. I tried to clean my shirt to no avail. I decided it would be best to pull off my bloody shirt and go home in my Tee-shirt. Bundling up the shirt and tie, I suddenly realized this was my favorite tie, given to me last Christmas—it was ruined. Darn!

I took my bloody bundle to my VW, threw it in the floorboard, and went back to my office for a final check. As I rounded the corner by the office, a television crew with a camera in hand almost ran me down. The media always monitored ambulance calls, and anytime an ambulance was sent to a school, they would dispatch reporters. They were in a hurry to make the evening news.

They rushed over to me, saying, "Are you a custodian? Can you tell us anything about the stabbing?"

As I was wearing an undershirt and khaki pants, they made the assumption that I was a custodian.

I replied, "The altercation took place on the second floor up those stairs to your left."

They immediately went to the stairs and found a few drops of blood. The blood spots were filmed. Their report was recorded with the stairs in the background. This would be on TV tonight.

The next day, we discovered the altercation was between the injured student and a short black student. I was told the white student considered himself somewhat of a martial arts expert. Both students' teachers had let them out of class a few minutes before the final bell. Their paths crossed, and words were exchanged. According to the investigation, the white student attack with a karate kick to the black student's chest. The kick knocked him back a few steps as the aggression continued. The smaller student reached into his back pocket and pulled out an Afro comb, a large metal comb eight to ten inches long with a wooden handle. The teeth are one-half inch apart and five inches long. The black student hit his aggressor several times with the Afro comb. The metal teeth sank deep into his chest, puncturing his lungs and neck.

The injured student did recover. Neither student was in my school jurisdiction, so I was not involved in the discipline. I never learned the disposition of the case, but I'm sure it was handled properly. At the meeting following the incident, the Nashville Board of Education outlawed metal Afro combs on school grounds.

JUST SPEND THE DAYS WITH ME

Every educator knows a major component for a student's success in school is strong parental support. This is also the reason that teachers and administrators call parents for their help when problems develop.

If students were sent to my office for a second time, it was a mandatory call to their parents. Most students did not want anyone from the school to call their parents. Ninety-five percent of my contacts with parents resulted in a positive response in the student's behavior. A school with three thousand enrollments made it impossible to know every family. The administrators unfortunately only got to know the students that were leaders or exceptional in their fields and those that had difficulty adjusting and needed help.

When a student continually refused to conduct himself properly, one of the steps to correct this problem was a parent conference. Demanding that the parents come to the school was a very effective disciplinary tool. They did not take the conference lightly as many had to leave work and sometimes lose a day's pay. Losing money added pressure on students to straighten up and fly right.

The major problem that I had with this procedure was not being equally fair to all parents. The majority of the black community lived several miles from the school, and many did not have transportation. When I called a black parent for a conference, they would often tell me they did not have transportation. I would ask them to talk with their son or daughter and convince them to improve. Sometimes this action was all that was needed.

When the phone call was not successful and the student still failed to cooperate, I would contact the parent again and tell them to keep their son or daughter home until they could come to the school. This usually created a hardship, having to get a friend to bring them to school or to take a taxi. This action often created the same result as in the white community; the major penalty was in the pocketbook. When the parents would not or could not come to the school, the final effort was to go see them.

There was one student, Razzell, who would not comply with any rules. When I suspended him and told him not to come back to school without his mother, he came to school anyway. I tried several times to call his mother, but the phone had been disconnected.

After exhausting every trick in my book, I looked at him as he sat calmly across from me and said, "We are going to take a little drive. I am taking you home, and we are going to see your mother."

The calm, cool attitude that he had previously displayed left his face and was replaced by a quizzical look and he said, "Say what?"

"Yep, Razzell, I have reached the end of my rope. We are going to see your mother."

His reply and attitude already changing as he said softly, "Yes, sir, when?"

I opened the desk drawer for my car keys. I looked him straight on and said, "Now."

I told my secretary where we were going. Razzell and I walked to my car, opened the door of my little sky-blue VW Rabbit, and crawled inside. He was still in disbelief as I started the car. It was not a short drive; Razzell lived in the inner city. Our conversation was nearly nil as we drove down the interstate.

He seemed almost like a caged animal, twisting and turning in his seat, wanting to get out of this situation and not knowing how.

As we approached the Murfreesboro Road exit, I looked over at my fidgeting, nervous passenger and said, "Where do you live? What's the address?"

I should have gotten the address before I left school, but I thought he would know where he lived. What I didn't foresee was that he had the information I needed, but he was reluctant to give it to me. We drove around in the low-income project area where he lived for about ten minutes.

He would tell me, "Turn right on this street and then turn left on that next street."

When we came down the same street for the second time, I realized that he was taking me on a merry chase.

I pulled the car over and said, "Razzell, either you show me how to get your house, or I will go to that phone booth, call the school, and get your address, or even better, ask one of your buddies walking down the street. I'm sure they know where you live."

That threat produced the response that I needed. We drove one block, turned right, and he pointed and said, "That's it."

I pulled the car to the curb and sat there just for a few seconds, contemplating what I might say to his mother.

Razzell made no effort to open the door; he just sat there until I said, "Let's go."

Then and only then did Razzell make any effort to move. As we got out of the car, the first thing glaring at us were three over-stuffed garbage bags on the front porch, blocking the door. Animals had torn into the bags, scattering food and trash across the porch. I kicked the trash off the porch. Razzell was standing at the base of the steps and had not moved.

He was still reluctant to go into the house, so I encouraged him with a firm, almost-commanding, "Let's go in."

With a deep breath, he took a key from around his neck, stepped over garbage left on the porch, and pushed open the sticking front door. As we entered the dingy, poorly kept room, an eerie feeling flooded my soul as if I was entering a forbidden area. I realized something was living here, but I was not sure what or how.

Located in the middle of the living room was a television, couch, and coffee table. On the coffee table were two half-empty cereal bowls with milk splattered beside them and spoons on the floor. A carton turned on its side had spilled milk across the table, leaving a large puddle on the floor. From the living room, I could see the sink piled high. Roaches were crawling on and around the pile of dirty dishes.

I glanced at Razzell. He was sitting on the couch with his head in his hands. It was obvious he was deeply affected by what was taking place.

"Razzell, I need to speak with your mother. Is she here?"

Without saying a word or even looking at me, he got up, opened the door across from the television, and disappeared into the next room.

A muffled, incoherent conversation emanated from the bedroom, "Who? What? What the hell.? Go away! Leave me the fuck alone."

After a few minutes of yelling and finally consoling, the door from the bedroom opened, and two figures emerged from the darkness. The person leaning on Razzell was small, about five feet two inches tall, slender, almost skinny, and was dressed in what looked like an old-tattered nightshirt. Her hair in the dim light looked as my dad would say, "A stump full of granddaddy long leg spiders."

In other words, a twisted mess of matted hair. With Razzell's help, his mother staggered into the living room and sat in the spilled milk on the coffee table. She looked at me and, with a very thick tongue, said, "What do you want?"

I tried to explain the situation and problems that we were having with Razzell, but she didn't appear to comprehend anything.

She looked up at me through dilated pupils and said, "Is that all? I am going back to bed."

Looking at this poor, emaciated person, I could only utter, "Yes, ma'am. That's all."

She slowly struggled to stand and begin to stumble back into the dark room from which she had come.

During my conference with Razzell's mother, he had gone into another room and closed the door. I got up and moved across the living room toward Razzell's room, carefully avoiding the milk and spoons.

I lightly tapped on the door and said, "Razzell, I need to talk with you."

I can still see him as he opened the door, standing in the dim light, his head hanging down, and his hand on the doorknob.

With a slight tug on his shoulder, I said, "Let's go back to school."

He looked at me and, with no effort to resist, moved toward the front door. We got into my car, started back to school, and rode in complete silence.

When we entered the school and went into my office, I said, "Razzell, we will have to work something else out on your suspension."

There was no reaction, facial or otherwise, from Razzell.

"I cannot let you go back into your classes because the teachers are expecting you to be suspended. The other students know about your behavior, and if you returned to school without punishment, they would expect the same leniency. Do you understand this?"

He nodded and replied, "Yes, I understand."

We came to an agreement that he would be suspended, but his suspension would not be at home. He was required to stay with me in my office for three days. Each of those three days would be spent sitting in my outer office and doing classwork teachers sent to him.

It may seem as if Razzell was getting off lightly. This was not the case; his peers discovered he had to spend three days sitting in my office doing schoolwork. They would go out of their way between classes to come by the office and razz him. Also, sitting for seven hours without interacting with other students and only your homework to occupy your time could be considered semisolitary confinement. This procedure was the forerunner of in-school suspension.

Lodged into my memory are those sights and smells of that day. If there is anything positive that came from the home visit and those suspension days, it was that Razzell was not sent to the office for the remainder of that school year. I'm not sure where Razzell is today, but I wish him well. He had a mountain to climb.

McGavock's Richie

I always tried to get to school early and plan my day before being overrun by hormonally enhanced teenagers. Entering the school through one of the twelve doors that led into the North-East cafeteria, I turned to look outside to see if the sun was going to come up. It was one of those days between winter and spring when the icy temperatures still had a grasp on the world, yet sprigs of grass and daffodils trying to break through the cold promised more pleasant weather in the near future. These small, almost obscure at times, signals sent from Mother Nature were enough to encourage us to continue the endless battle against ignorance.

The cold still sending shivers down my back, I decided to go to the North office, where Mrs. Rob McGee, the guidance counselor, always kept a pot of hot coffee. I knew the coffee would be ready because Mrs. McGee came to school early. I would sneak in the front way to the North office so she could not see me and borrow a cup of coffee. She would apprehend me at various times and got better as a coffee cop as the year progressed. At each apprehension, I would be fined and forced to donate to her coffee fund. As the year passed, my confiscations became more numerous, and the cost of her coffee fines increased. The fun cat-and-mouse coffee game became expensive. I found it more financially feasible to buy a coffeepot and brew coffee in my office. The coffee wasn't quite as good as Mrs. McGee's, but I did not have to endure the fines and her lighthearted, embarrassing tongue-lashing when she caught me.

On this particular day, the chill was still in the air, and about midmorning, I needed another cup of coffee. I decided to risk being caught for that extra cup. While sneaking past the ever-vigilant Mom McGee and pouring my coffee, I overheard the North school secretary's phone conversation. She mentioned the notorious Richie Smith. Even though McGavock High School was only three years old, Richie Smith was almost a legend among the administrators. He was a special education student and had a mind that went in variously wild directions.

One of his favorite activities was to find a group of pretty young ladies talking and laughing during lunch. Richie would slowly blend in with these girls and casually pretend to be listening.

Before the girls realized that Richie was among them, he would look at the girls and say, "This is for y'all."

He would then raise his leg and take the stance of a junkyard dog that had just discovered a rival had been leaving markings in his territory. Richie would smile and then release the most obnoxious, penetrating, loud, low-hanging, nauseating combination of intestinal gases that had ever scorched this earth. The girls would scatter, and Richie would laugh. He could have easily been considered a weapon of mass destruction during World War I. At any rate, he had made several visits to Mr. Currie, the North school principal.

Taking my first sip of coffee, I overheard Mr. Currie's secretary explaining to the person on the phone, "Yes, sir. He attends school here, but I cannot give out that information unless I know who you are."

The voice on the phone identified himself as Richie Smith's father. I heard the secretary reply, "Just one moment please. Let me check." She put the individual on hold and quickly moved from her chair to Mr. Currie's office door.

Opening the door, and in an inpatient voice, she said, "Mr. Currie, Mr. Currie, I think Richie Smith is on the phone, and he is on the absentee list."

Mr. Currie asked, "What line?"

The secretary did not reply. She just punched the correct line and handed Mr. Currie the telephone. It appeared that Richie was checking to see if the school knew he was absent or, in this case, skipping school.

Mr. Currie took the phone and said, "This is James Currie, principal of the North school. Can I help you?"

The voice on the phone replied with his best mature masculine voice, "This is Richie Smith's father. Is Richie at school today?"

Having dealt with Richie many times, Mr. Currie recognized his voice immediately and said, "Richie! Richie Smith! Is that you, boy? You better get yourself back to school before we send the police after you."

The person on the phone suddenly became silent for a few seconds before a reply was uttered, "Uh, uh, uh, no, Mr. Currie. This is not me."

Richie did get to school before eleven o'clock. He handed the secretary an excuse supposedly signed by his mother. Richie was one of the many unique students that we had the opportunity to experience.

INDUSTRIAL HAND WASHER

McGavock was the newest and largest school in the state of Tennessee. The building and equipment was state of the art, both functionally and educationally. The major halls were over ten feet wide, and the floors were made of forever-lasting terrazzo. Terrazzo is made of chips of marble, quartz, granite, glass, and other suitable material poured with a cementitious binder. The mixture is smoothed and allowed to dry. The terrazzo is then polished to a high gloss. It was expensive, but the low maintenance and durability made it cost-effective.

The restrooms were also modern. Located in each restroom were two large concrete composite terrazzo industrial hand washers. They were semicircular with the flat side attached neatly to the wall. Each was four feet wide and two feet deep with soap dispensers and paper towel containers on the wall. At the base of each sink was a round black bar that students would press with their foot to allow water to flow like a spring shower from the top of the sink for washing hands. The facility was well designed and functional.

I had never seen an industrial hand-wash sink in a school before, and apparently, some students had not either. Between classes, teachers and administrators would go into restrooms to prevent all types of unsavory activities, such as smoking, bullying, and gambling. The major gambling activity at this time was called pitching pennies. Kids would pitch coins toward the wall. The person's coin closest to the wall without touching it would win all the pitched coins. If quarters were used and there were five or six people in the game, a person would win several dollars in a short time if he were good or very lucky. One student consistently winning could cause tempers to flare, resulting in a fight. Regular restroom visitations by teachers kept gambling and smoking to a minimum.

Early in the year, I would make restroom checks during lunch period to set a trend so students knew I was in the area. Entering the restroom, I had to take a second look at what I saw. Four black students were standing at urinal position, peeing in the industrial hand washer. It looked somewhat humorous, four young adults urinating in the sink.

When I saw them, I said, "What are you fellows doing?"

The looks and mumbling they gave made me realize that I could have chosen a better comment.

"Man, we're taking a piss" was the first reply, followed by, "Move over, dude, and let him join us. He must be busting." Then a roar of laughter and one-handed high-fives erupted.

I laughed with them and said, "Okay, fellows, put 'em in your pants and come with me."

This caused another onslaught of gripes and unsavory comments.

"Man, we ain't done nothing wrong."

"You taking us to the office?"

"We waz just leaking."

"Just hold your horses and follow me."

"Oh, de word is out 'bout our horses."

This caused another scoring session, "That's right, man. We got big horses."

It was not my day for politically correct conversation. I quickly headed toward the back of the restroom and around the block partition that separated the handwashing area from the toilet facilities, telling them again, "Y'all come with me."

Going toward the back of the restroom, rather than the door, created other remarks, "Where we going? Dis white dude is crazy."

I rounded the corner where you could see the line of toilet stalls. When the group caught up with me, I did not say a word, just pointed to the six urinals located on the wall across from the toilets.

They looked at me, and a few replies came forth, "Oh, I didn't know," and still trying to be cool, continued, "Just look, a stall for each of our horses. Haha."

"Now you know," I said while moving from the back section of the restroom toward the door. I was feeling pretty good about confronting a problem, solving it, and educating students in a fundamental life skill.

While patting myself on the back, I started out the door, making one last backward glance. I stopped in my tracks. There it was. I could not believe it—teaching two life-skill lessons in one day.

At the washbasin were two white kids, one tall and the other super short, about five feet tall, standing on his tip toes to pee in the sink. Their life skills seemed to be a little more advanced than the first group. The tall student had discovered the foot pedal and was squirting water into the sink while they were peeing.

I wheeled around, remembering my previous mistakes, and said, "Fellows, we need to talk for a minute."

Even though the handwashing facilities were the same, we never had that problem with the girls' restroom. I guess women are just smarter.

What's in a Name

It was another day at the hormone-infested school where I was principal. The spring weather was causing the birds to chirp, flowers to bloom, and the dogwood trees were budding. To me, that meant the crappie would start biting. I had a weeklong fishing trip planned for spring break next week.

That was my take on spring. The students had a different slant on the season. Girls seemed to be wearing their clothes tighter and shorter while the boys were walking in circles, trying to get the courage to approach the cutie-pie of his choice. Books, grades, even food was taking a back seat to the seasonal mating process.

Occasionally, two young men would have their attention focused on the same damsel. This dual attention sometime caused sparks to fly. Such was the case on this day.

The final cafeteria feeding frenzy had ended, and the hormonally enhanced students were finding their way to the fifth-period class. Leaving the office, I was heading to the T, a place where three halls joined together, to observe student movement. Rounding the corner before reaching the T, I found three students mouthing at each other.

The taller of the two was loudly spewing out profanity, saying, "You, you, sorry son of a bitch, I better not catch you."

The shorter and more firmly built of the three and the receiver of the profanity replied, "I am going to beat the hell out of you."

The third was plump, with his shirttail pulled out, sweating and standing between the two potential gladiators. It was all he could do to keep the two apart as he yelled, "Come on, fellows! This is crazy."

When he saw me suddenly appear, the rotund peacemaker said in a loud clear voice, "Oh shit."

That was about the way I felt too. Two more hours, and it would have been a good day.

I grabbed the two combatants by their arms and gave them a firm jerk. The jerk along with them, catching a glimpse of my tie, caused a calming of the potentially bloody battle.

"Fellows, let's go to my office."

Getting the fighters out of the hall and away from the prying eyes of other students was my first priority.

As we started to the office, the chubby peacemaker began to move away as if he was not involved.

"Hey, you come with us," I said.

His comment was, "I was not fighting."

"No, you come with me. I may need you to explain why this happened."

He turned, mumbled something under his breath, and headed our way.

When in the office, I sat them in chairs the same way I found them in the hall. The two fighters were placed on each side of the desk with the uninvolved overweight, shirttail-out student sitting between them. Unfortunately, I did not know these students. I looked at each student for a few seconds then walked to the window and looked out long enough for them to regain their breath and composure. Looking out the window at the greening grass and blooming flowers sent my mind to fishing for those slab crappie on Kentucky Lake. That thought poured over my body and calmed me, like rubbing Bengay on a sore muscle.

Turning to the three, I said, "Okay, fellows, I need your names, and then we will see what this is all about."

Both fighters still had scowls on their faces, which negated the crappie effect that I had just enjoyed and needed. I began to settle back into my tense-iterated self that comes over me each time I have to deal with a fight.

Starting left to right, I asked, "What is your name?"

The tallest of the three with a belligerent look on his face said, "Cony."

Waiting for a few seconds for a last name that never came, I asked, "You got a last name?"

Having to pull obvious information out of him was beginning to grate on my nerves like fingernails across a caulk board.

His comment was "Yes."

Still, he offered no last name. Cony was not making it easy for himself or me. I had all I could take from this arrogant, tall drink of water.

"What is your last name?" I asked more sternly.

He said, "Roney."

"Your name is Cony Roney?" I exclaimed.

"That's right," he smartly replied.

That was the last straw. "Cony Roney, huh?" as I stood up and started around my desk to get to him and said, "I want your real name."

It was bad enough that I had to force him to give his name, but giving a false rhyming name was too much. Just as I was moving around the desk, Cony began to slide his chair away from me toward the corner of the room.

This is when the peacemaker, Ron, stood up and said in a frightful, high-pitched voice, "Dr. Hargis, that is his real name, and his brother's name is Macki."

Stopping in my tracks, I said, "What? Macki Roney?"

I looked at Cony and said, "Is that right? Your brother's name is Macki Roney?"

He replied with an affirmative nod.

My head, still spinning, I said, "Really?"

All three said, "Yes, sir. That's true."

I smiled to myself and thought, *There are times when the unexpected can put a new stress-relieving perspective on the entire situation.* This information added a little misguided humor to my inner being.

After mentally digesting these names, I asked, "Why the fight?"

They all started to speak at once. "Wait a minute, I want to hear from Ron. He was trying to keep you fellows from fighting. Ron, tell me straight. What really happened?"

Ron said, "Both Cony and Bill are dating the same girl, and they heard that she liked Bill better than Cony."

"Who told you she said that?" I inquired.

They all looked at one another, and after giving inquisitive looks and shoulder shrugs, they said, "We don't know for sure. Ron said he heard it."

"I overheard it in the lunch line. Not sure which of the girls in front of me said it," Ron replied.

"Fellows, you don't know who said what or if it is true. You two could beat each other bloody, and it will still be her decision who she likes. Are you going to let hearsay and a girl get you suspended? Is she worth that?"

They each slowly shook their heads no.

I looked at Cony and said, "Do you think you can keep a cool head on your shoulders for the rest of the week, at least until spring break?"

Cony's reply was "Yes, sir."

"How about it, Ron, Bill, can you do the same?"

Both nodded.

"Since there was not a fight, just an almost fight, I am going to let you slide this time," I said, slowly looking at each boy.

"Bill, you and Cony need to thank Ron for stopping the fight. Otherwise, you would be facing a ten-day suspension," I lectured.

I wrote them a note to get in class, and as they were leaving, I said, "Don't let those girls get you in any more trouble"

They took their notes with a relieved expression, shaking their heads affirmatively and headed to class.

Recording the incident on my three-by-five index card filing system, I chuckled and said to myself, "Cony Roney and Macki Roney, what a hoot. Something to tell my fishing buddies next week."

Student Referrals

All principals, and especially assistant principals, know that one of their major jobs is student discipline. Everyone is in agreement—parents, teachers, and even students—that if discipline is not maintained in the classroom, learning will come to a halt. The general policy in most schools is that teachers are responsible for maintaining discipline within their classrooms. If disruptive behavior comes to the point that the teacher cannot manage the student, that student is sent to the office with a referral slip, explaining the situation. The teacher is basically saying to the principal that this student's behavior is beyond my ability to manage, and I need help.

This standard policy functions well as most teachers do a good job in student management. There are always a few teachers who do not have the ability to manage students and even antagonize them at times. At McGavock High School, I was in charge of the east portion of the student body, which consisted of approximately eight hundred students and forty-three teachers. Under normal condition, this student population was considered high for only one administrator. If each teacher sent in only one referral a day, there would be forty-three referrals or two hundred fifteen per week. Thank the good Lord and competent teachers, that did not occur.

All schools have a few teachers who are overactive in sending referrals to the office. Two such teachers were on my staff. We had seminars concerning classroom management with little success. Also, individual teacher's conferences were not effective, as most teachers who lacked the ability to manage their classroom think that it is not their lack of skill, but the problem is disruptive students. Something had to be done; in other words, they were wearing me out.

A plan was devised to make teachers aware of the number of referrals that were sent to the office. This was to be implemented during in-service just prior to the starting of the second semester. The first task was to count all the referrals that had been sent to the office the first semester. The number was surprisingly large. The second task was to total the number of referrals that came from each teacher. A plan was developed in which each teacher could see their number of discipline referrals without any of the other teachers knowing.

We gave each teacher a personal identification number. Then we gave out a sheet of paper, listing all the discipline referral numbers corresponding to the teacher identification number. It caused quite a stir. There were two teachers that had sent over one hundred referrals to the office in one semester. That totaled more than one referral per day. No faculty member knew who those two teachers were because the teacher identification numbers were secret.

One teacher taking a hard look at the totals said, "Is this correct or a typo?"

My reply was "Everything you see is correct."

The response was "Surely, this wrong."

"No, everything is accurate. We double-checked it."

The interesting result of this procedure was a reduction in student referrals from those two teachers. The reduction was 40 percent for one teacher and almost 60 percent for the other. Peer pressure actually caused the reduction in referrals and improved classroom management for these teachers even though their peers did not know who they were.

The improvement was due to self-imposed peer pressure and the fear that this activity would be standard operating procedure for future faculty meetings. We never had to do it again.

Cohn High School

STARTING FROM SCRATCH

The Nashville school system had been functioning under a desegregation plan for ten years. In 1981, an appeal was approved by a federal
judge. The school system was forced to return to the original zones
until a new plan could be approved. This included opening and closing several schools and reassigning large numbers of students. The
plaintiffs were not satisfied with the lower court's decision and had
filed an appeal with a higher court. Suddenly in 1981, with no warn-
ing, the higher court handed down a decision and upheld the appeal
shortly before the opening of school. The appellate judge reversed
the decision of the lower court. The school system was ordered to
return to the original status until an acceptable plan could be developed. Students had to be reassigned; schools reopened and properly
furnished within two weeks.

The judge had the right to reverse the lower court desegregation
plan, but I will never understand the timing in handing down his
decision. There was no time allowed for planning. The judge's order
was *do it now!* This added more chaos for an already-disturbed school
system.

Not being aware of the decision that had been handed down,
I was in my office well prepared for the opening of school. I was
leaning back in my chair with my feet resting on my desk, and as it
always seems when you are in a comfortable position, mentally or
physically, something or somebody always interrupts your serenity.

The phone rang. My boss was calling. He said, "There has been a
change in the federal court order, and schools will not be opening for
two weeks. We are forced to go back to the former school zoning pattern. I am calling to offer you the principalship of Cohn High School if
you are interested. According to the judge, Cohn has to be reopened."

I asked, "How much time do I have to make a decision?"

My answer seemed to irritate him, and his reply was "About ten minutes."

I said, "Okay, I will call you back shortly and let you know."

I went directly over to the executive principal, Dr. Howard Baltimore, who had replaced retired principal, Mr. Chester Lafever. After explaining my phone call, I said, "What do you think?"

His comment was "Do what you want to do."

Looking back on the situation, I'm sure that he had been contacted and knew what the central office was planning. I guess my visit to him was a courtesy call even though, at the time, I did not view it that way. I thought he might give me some insight and advice, which did not come forth.

I called my boss and said, "I accept the job."

He replied, "Fine, you need to know that you have one week to get the school in order and ready for the students."

That evening, while sitting on the deck watching the sunset, I began to realize the task set before me. One major problem was no furniture for high school students. The school had been furnished with middle school desks and tables. The high school desk and tables had been sent to Hillwood High School. The only bright spot that I could think of was that the high school desk that were formerly at Cohn were new. They had been brought for the school the last year just prior to its closing.

I contacted the maintenance department about bringing the desks back to Cohn. They informed me that they were in the process of getting the desks and would deliver them in the next couple of days. True to his word, two days later, the trucks arrived filled with desks. The maintenance department employees, along with our custodians and me, began to unload the truck. To my dismay, there was not one new desk taken off the trucks. The new ones had remained at Hillwood.

I asked, "Where are the new desks that were taken from Cohn?"

The foreman of the maintenance crew just looked at me, shrugged his shoulders, and said, "This is what they told me to bring to Cohn."

Time was of the essence, so I did not have the time to find out who made the decision to keep the new furniture and to raise the devil about it.

The second and probably more important task was getting a schedule for all the incoming students. When you have approximately seven hundred students entering the building with no schedules or plans for them, this could be an open opportunity for chaos. The first thing I did was meet with the guidance counselors and several teachers to outline a plan for scheduling the students and agree on rooms to use as headquarters. Counselors and selected teachers were helpful and competent. I think most of the teachers and all the students were happy to have Cohn reopened.

When the students entered the building, we directed them to the auditorium and divided them alphabetically into homerooms. Teachers escorted the students to their classroom, where they filled out information cards that would be used throughout the year. The next problem was scheduling the students in an orderly manner. Things moved slowly but effectively.

The guidance counselors decided to schedule the seniors first, juniors, sophomores, and finally, the freshman. They would come to the guidance headquarters by homerooms. One of the paramount problems was the boring time for those students that were sitting in the homeroom. The scheduling process was going to take two, maybe three days. Sitting in homerooms all day with nothing to do can increase anxiety, tempers, and result in problems.

The auditorium was large enough to accommodate the majority of the students, and we were fortunate that the Nashville school system had a very comprehensive film library. I called the librarian supervisor, explained our situation to her, and asked, "What full-length movies do you have that would interest high school students?"

Fortunately, her reply was "We have just purchased five full-length movies that should be what you need."

Excitedly, I said, "Please hold all of those films for me."

She said, "I will hold four. One has already been sent out. I will put them on delivery."

"No," I replied. "I am on my way to get them."

After obtaining the full-length films and setting up the projector, we asked all the students in the ninth, tenth, and eleventh grades to report the auditorium. As the students moved into the auditorium guided by their homeroom teachers, the smell of freshly popped popcorn filled the air. The popcorn was going to cause a mess, but I always felt that if a person is satisfying a basic human need, there was a less likely chance of disruptive activity.

We sold large bags of popcorn for ten cents. That covered our cost and put a little money in the general fund, which was badly needed, as there was zero money in the school account.

After three days of scheduling, the guidance counselors were thoroughly exhausted but did an exceptional job. I'm sure I expressed myself inadequately at the time, but I'll always be indebted to the competency and hard work of the guidance counselors and teachers at Cohn High School. They turned a very difficult and possibly disastrous situation into a smoothly oiled registration process.

After three days of registration, Cohn began a regular schedule and an interesting year.

A Visit from a Local Legend

After accepting the position as principal of Cohn High School, I was told to expect a visit from a former principal of Cohn. He was principal from 1939 to 1965. He and his wife still lived in the community and were highly respected. The advice given to me was to listen to him, but do not let him run the school. The problems with opening a school almost from scratch left little time to be concerned about a visit from a former principal.

In a few weeks, my secretary received a phone call, letting us know that Mr. Rochelle would be coming tomorrow at ten o'clock. One thing that stood out to me was that he did not ask for an appointment, he was coming at ten o'clock, and I was expected to be there. After the advice that I had received and information learned from the community, it would be best that I receive him at ten o'clock.

Mr. Rochelle came to the school at precisely ten o'clock.

We shook hands, and I said, "It is a pleasure to meet you, Mr. Rochelle. I have heard a great deal about you."

His reply was "You should not believe everything that you hear."

"Have a seat."

Watching closely where he sat, I pulled my chair to the side so the desk would not be between us. Some theories consider the desk a barrier for positive communication.

He said, "I am glad to see Cohn reopened, and it should have never been closed."

We both agreed on that concept as Cohn High School had the exact black-to-white ratio of 20 percent, which was what the court had ordered the school system to accomplish. The 20 percent black/white ratio was the reflection of the Nashville community.

As we talked and laughed a little, I asked, "What were some more memorable problems that took place with students while you were principal?"

Mr. Rochelle put his hand to his chin as his mind scanned through his twenty-five-plus years.

He said, "One of the biggest problems we had back in those days was keeping students from smoking on school grounds."

The Cohn building was located on one city block and was completed surrounded by homes. There was a public park directly across the street that was used for school activities. The football field was located about five minutes away on the other side of the interstate.

I asked, "Where did they smoke? The restrooms?"

He smiled and said, "A lot of them would sneak off campus and go into the garages of the homes across the street. Occasionally, some homeowners would catch them and chase them back to the school. Then they would call me."

A big grin came across his face that quickly deteriorated into a disgusting look while shaking his head.

"I remember this one case," he said, "some students went across the street and hid in a garage to smoke. Apparently, they left in a big hurry and did not put their cigarettes out properly. They caught the garage on fire."

To me, this was very serious and took me by surprise.

I asked, "Mr. Rochelle, what did you do? Call the police? Or turn the kids over to the fire marshal?"

With a grin on his face, he replied, "I brought them into the office, tanned their hides, called their parents, and told them they had a garage to pay for."

I couldn't help but laugh, thinking about how times had changed and how acceptable procedures for handling disciplinary problems had evolved.

Mr. Rochelle looked at his watch and said, "I have taken up enough of your time. If I can help, don't hesitate to call me."

We shook hands, and he exited my office, speaking to students and secretaries as he left. Pulling my chair around behind my desk, I sat down, looked around the office, and watched students moving to their classes. I wondered just how many lives Mr. Rochelle had impacted positively. I liked Mr. Rochelle and knew he would be an asset rather than a deterrent for me. I told a friend, Tom Shacklett, director of computer services for the Metro School System, about meeting Mr. Rochelle. Tom graduated from Cohn and had a few stories to tell me about Mr. Rochelle.

Andy Holt, the president of the University of Tennessee, and Mr. Rochelle were personal friends. Mr. Rochelle called on him many times to help deserving students find funds to attend college.

One story that Tom related reflected the intellect and social psychology that Mr. Rochelle used to encourage and get the best efforts from students. There was one individual that was going to school at the same time that Tom attended Cohn. This student was highly intelligent but a real goof-off. He was in and out of the office on a regular basis. Mr. Rochelle was constantly encouraging and pushing him in every way he knew. Apparently, he had told the student that he was not going to amount to anything.

Several years after this roguish individual graduated from Cohn, he received a medical doctor's degree from the University of Tennessee. He made a point to come by and see Mr. Rochelle. He was dressed in an expensive suit and looked successfully sharp. It was to be a "look at me now" visit.

The former underachieving Cohn student walked into Mr. Rochelle's office and said, "You remember me and when you told me I had the ability, but I was not going to amount to anything? Do you remember that? Well, I just came by to let you know that you were wrong. I am a doctor."

Mr. Rochelle stood up, walked around his desk, shook the young man's hand, and said, "Congratulations. I am glad to know that my plan worked."

The young man looked at Mr. Rochelle with a surprised and puzzled look, hesitated, and said, "Thank you."

He turned and walked out of the office.

My last personal encounter with Mr. Rochelle was in the hospital. A teacher came by the office and informed me that he was in the hospital and suggested we go to see him. He had surgery, and it was questionable if he would leave the hospital. Entering his room, I found him in the typical hospital bed with the head slightly raised. Tubes and wires were attached to every part of his body.

I said, "Mr. Rochelle, we wanted to come by to wish you the best. I know you'll improve and be home soon."

He looked up, reached out and, took my hand, pulled me closer to him, and in a weak voice, said, "Thank you for coming to see me. I want you to know that I am very happy that you are at Cohn High School."

He let go of my hand, settled back into his pillow, and closed his eyes. The nurse at the foot of his bed said, "It's best you go now."

Mr. Rochelle did recover and returned to his home shortly after our visit. I talked with him by phone several times after his hospital stay, but he never seemed to have the same vitality that he had prior to entering the hospital. I have often thought about his comment to me. From a personal standpoint, it is probably one of the most appreciated compliments that I ever received. Mr. Rochelle was not only a good principal but a great man.

AN ALMOST RIOT

The year was progressing smoothly, and to my surprise, our sports program was doing well. Coach Bozeman's football team had a winning season and both basketball teams were improving rapidly and appeared they might get to the regional tournament. I was particularly pleased with the girls' team's improvement and attributed their success to Coach Pope and a group of girls that worked very hard. The girls made it to the regional tournament and the boys to the sub-state.

Coach Vaughan's basketball team relied heavily on one player. He was a good, somewhat of a showboat, and spent little time on the books. He was college material, but I was not sure that his grades would allow him to get a scholarship. We had two games left in the regular season before tournaments began. Our schedule was somewhat spotty, as we had to accept any school that had an open date, due to the sudden reopening of Cohn.

Our next game was at Page High School in Williamson County. The boys' basketball team was mostly white. Their side of the gymnasium was 95 percent white while our side of the bleachers was evenly distributed salt and pepper. The game was nip and tuck. The tension was rising in the players. The officials did a good job keeping the lid on this pressure cooker that was slowly coming to a boil. We were ahead a few points as the seconds were ticking away.

Then suddenly, out of nowhere, a Page player came up behind our star and pushed him in the back, almost knocking him to the floor. The Cohn player managed to keep his balance and aggressively turned around to find his attacker. This was just the kind of action that we did not need. The officials blew their whistles as the players started at each other. The coaches, police officers, basketball officials, and school administrators began separating the combative players.

One of the officials acted intelligently and blew his whistle and said, "This game is over!"

Both officials left the floor, and the Cohn coach told his players to go to their dressing room. Fortunately, the players did exactly as they were told.

After we cleared the gymnasium floor, I went to the Cohn dressing room. I was expecting to see a group of players huffing, puffing, cursing, and wanting to retaliate. Mentally, I was planning my speech to the players and coaches on how we would handle this situation. When I opened the dressing room door, there was no noise, no players, no towels, no nothing; the dressing room was completely empty. My first thought was, *This is the wrong dressing room.*

Going back to the gymnasium, I saw a Page assistant principal. Being upset about the situation, I may have spoken to him in a too forcible manner when I asked, "Where did you put the Cohn players?"

He was not in a good mood either and came back at me rather abruptly, "I didn't put them anywhere. They used that dressing room over there," pointing as he spoke.

"They are not there. Are you sure it was that dressing room?"

He gave me that just get-the-hell-out-of-here look and said, "Yes, that's the dressing room."

Before I could reply, our scorekeeper grabbed my arm and said, "Our coach and players have already left."

"Great! That's good to know."

The coach had told the players when they entered the dressing room, "Grab your things and run to the cars. You can dress in the car or when we get back to the school."

He had made a wise decision and probably kept the situation from escalating.

Knowing the Cohn players were safe, I looked around the gym for the Page principal. I found him near the door, talking with a group of parents. After he calmed the parents and they began to leave, I approached him.

"Do you know what caused the pushing and shoving?"

He said, "I don't know. I will call you tomorrow after I talk with the coach."

I replied, "Thanks, I will do the same," and eagerly left the building.

Early the next morning, I received a call, not from Page's principal but from Mr. Gideon, the executive director of the Tennessee Secondary School Athletic Association (TSSAA). The officials were very efficient in reporting the possible riot. Mr. Gideon asked, "What in the world happened?"

I explained, "A Page player pushed a Cohn player in the back during the closing seconds of the game. I was watching the game, and I did not see our player provoke anyone. The Page principal will call me today and inform me of the results of his investigation. I will be doing my own here at Cohn."

"Let me know what you find out," he replied.

After talking with the TSSAA, I summoned our coach to my office.

He explained, "The team told me they did not know why the Page player pushed Reggie. One comment was the white team did not like being beat by a black team and started the fight."

Our star player stated emphatically, "I didn't do nothing."

I completed my investigation and was waiting for the report from the principal of Page. That call came at 10:30 a.m.

He said, "According to our player, your player tripped and elbowed him on the other end of the court after that last rebound. Our player is trustworthy, and I believe him."

I replied, "That leaves us in a dilemma because our players said they didn't do anything wrong."

The Page principal said, "We might have a way to solve this problem. The basketball game was taped by a local cable TV company for viewing later during the week."

"Have you seen the tape?"

"No, I have not, but I will pick it up and look at it later this week."

"Where is this TV station? If they will let me borrow the tape, I will pick it up today."

He gave me the phone number and directions to the television station. I drove to Franklin and got the tape.

Exiting the station door, I heard, "Bring that tape back as soon as you can! We want to air it this week."

I said, "This shouldn't take long. Hopefully, it will be back to you tomorrow."

The VCR market was just beginning to blossom, and very few people had one. We did not have a VCR tape player at school because they were too expensive. When I returned to school, I asked several teachers if they had one or knew where a tape player might be available. Most of the teachers just politely smiled and shook their heads no.

The smile actually said, "Do you think I can afford one of those?"

My secretary, Mrs. Leaming, was always on the ball and suggested that I walk across the park to Charlotte Avenue and inquire if a business might have one. My first stop was a furniture/appliance store. Lo and behold, what did I see in the window, a VCR- and television-playing a tape. I entered the building and asked for the manager.

The gentleman's reply was "I am the owner. What can I do for you?"

"I am the principal of Cohn High School, and I have a tape of one our basketball games and would like to view it for just a few minutes."

"Sure," and took the tape from me and placed it in the VCR.

I explained, "I only need to see the last few minutes."

He fast-forwarded the tape to the last minutes of the game, and I started watching closely. I was extremely disappointed at what I saw. The Page player had told the truth. Our star player had pushed him during a rebound and then elbowed him while he was returning to the other end of the court. Our player had bold-faced lied to us. It was the second time I had been truly angry while at Cohn; I was livid.

When I returned to the school, my first action was to call the principal at Page and express my regrets and apologies to him and his team.

I told him, "I would take care the matter."

My second task was to call Mr. Gideon at the TSSAA. "I am apologizing to you for the actions of one of our players."

We discussed the matter for a few minutes, and he said, "What are you planning to do?"

Having a good relationship with Mr. Gideon, I told him, "I will take care of the matter, and the guilty player will not be playing for a couple of games."

This was good enough for Mr. Gideon, and he asked me to write a report and give him the details.

I called our coach to my office and explained to him what had taken place. He did not seem very surprised, which made me think he might have known. One game remained in the regular season before we entered the district tournament.

I explained to the player, "Because of your dishonesty and poor sportsmanship, you will not play in the next two games. Not only will you not participate in the games, you can't dress out in your uniform. You will sit on the bench wearing your street clothes."

This was the most embarrassing and devastating punishment that I could think of to give him without removing him from the team. When he was not in uniform, everyone would ask questions. Word got around quickly that he had screwed up.

I'm not sure that he learned anything from this situation and punishment. He got a college basketball scholarship but was dismissed from the team due to his lack of interest in academia. It was sad that he lost the chance for a college education.

THE SNOW OF 1981

It was just before lunch, and the forecast for the night was approximately three to four inches of snow. The probability of snow causes an undue restlessness among students. In every class, while the teachers were lecturing, the students' eyes were focused on the windows. When are the first flakes going to fall? I was not too concerned about the snow catching us at school because the weather bureau reported that the snow would be coming in late evening.

But just to be on the financially safe side, the central office food division asked schools to be sure that students were served lunch even if we had to allow them to eat early. Allowing students to eat early would ensure that the cafeteria would not have leftovers and wasted food. The food division of the school system is self-supporting and receives no funds from the general school system budget. Losing the revenue for one day could have a devastating effect. We had just fed our last group of students, and I had returned to my office.

From the window, the gray snow clouds could be seen slowly sliding across the sky. Occasionally, there would be a crack in the clouds that allowed a shot of sunbeams to briefly reflect off the tree limbs and bounce to the ground. The sun slipping through the dark clouds almost seemed to say, *don't despair. There's always hope.* Sitting at my desk with one eye on the students, moving and chatting in the hall as they changed classes, and the other eye on those increasingly menacing clouds, my concern began to build. I kept the weather radio on the table close to my desk in case there were warnings of impending dangerously inclement weather. The weather radio was still predicting heavy snow to reach Nashville in the late evening or night.

The mounting intensity of the clouds began to worry me enough that I called the central office and asked, "Can we possibly have permission to turn school out early? These clouds are as black as an ace of spades."

I was told, "We are going to stay until dismissal time."

Our librarian was watching our only television, and the forecast was just a little different. They were still reporting heavy snows in the late afternoon and early night, but they also said that snow was coming down rather hard in Dickson. Waiting to dismiss students from school at the normal time was beginning to make less sense to me. Dickson was only twenty-five miles from Nashville as the crow flies, and according to the weather bureau, there was a westerly wind of fifteen-plus miles per hour. School was normally dismissed at two o'clock, and it was presently 12:00 p.m.—that left two hours for us to remain in school. According to my calculations, heavy snow from Dickson would reach our school in less than two hours because we were located on the west side of Nashville. If the calculations were accurate, we could be sitting in school for thirty minutes, watching snow accumulate.

It was pushing one o'clock, and I could see fifty-cent-size snow-flakes sporadically dropping from the sky. They were pretty, but there was trouble in each flake. I called the central office again and asked, "Are we going to dismiss school early?"

I got the same reply, "No, the snow will be here late this after-noon. We will have time to get the kids home."

Looking out the window while talking with the central office, the snowflakes were beginning to get larger and coming down more profusely.

I asked again, "Are you sure? We got snowflakes coming down here, large enough to cover my Volkswagen bug."

The answer was blunt and cold, "I told you once. We will dis-miss at the regular time. You hear!"

Once again, I was ticked off. The snow was coming down hard, and I just couldn't keep the students in school any longer. We were fortunate that Cohn was truly a community school and only had two buses. The remainder of the students walked to school. Apparently, the school bus drivers were in the same mind-set. They arrived about the time my last phone call to the central office was completed. The buses were an hour early.

I went outside and asked the drivers, "Are you ready to load the students and get on the road?"

The two drivers, one lady and one gentleman, replied in the following order, "Yes!" and "Hell yes! I should have already been half-way through my route."

"We will load the kids in five minutes."

My comments were short and to the point over the public address system. "May I have your attention please. Due to the snow, we're going to dismiss school an hour early. Those students who are bus riders will be dismissed first. When the buses are loaded, we will dismiss the rest of the students."

The buses were loaded in less than ten minutes.

When I returned to the intercom, I said, "The remainder of the students are dismissed. Students, be careful going home. It appears to be very slick. Teachers, as soon as your students clear your classroom, you are free to go home. Be careful. The snow is beginning to stick on the roads."

It was approximately 1:15 p.m., and the school had been cleared. I put on my coat and got everything ready for my twenty-mile trek home through snow and stalled cars. Just as I started out the door, the phone rang. My first thought was, *Do I answer the phone? It can only be trouble!* Then I realized we are not out of school according to the central office. I picked up the phone and said, "Cohn High School." It was trouble. A stranded teacher.

She said in a frightened, disgusted voice, "My car is in the ditch. Is anyone at school coming toward West End Avenue? I really need a ride."

I said, "No one is here, but I can come by and try to help you. Maybe we can get your car out of the ditch. I will be there in a few minutes."

No sooner had I hung up the phone when it rang again. Another teacher needed help. Fortunately, they were both in the same general area. I told the second teacher, "I will be there shortly."

My thought process was that we could get their cars going again in a short period, and then I could drive home. Mistake. The first car was in the ditch with a front wheel completely off the ground; the car was beyond our help. The teacher squeezed in my VW, and we headed to the second car. Reaching it, we found that all three of us could not push the car back up on the road.

We reentered the VW bug, and I said, "Where do you live? I'll take you home."

My short Good Samaritan act turned into three hours. Both teachers lived in opposite directions, and I neglected to calculate the slow-moving cars on the streets. By the time I had deposited both teachers at their homes, darkness was spreading across the landscape. The dim light and heavy snow made visibility difficult. The VW bug had done well on the snowy roads. The major problem was stalled vehicles that were difficult to maneuver around.

My journey home was not going to be easy as it was still snowing, and the temperature was dropping. The windshield wipers were beginning to freeze and were becoming useless. Visibility was nil from the driver's seat. Sticking my head out the window to drive was not satisfactory because it only took seconds for my glasses to be covered with snow. Lights were visible in the automotive parts store ahead on the right. Sliding into the parking lot, I went inside and purchased their last spray can of deicer. I thought, *This might do the job.* With the deicer in my left hand and driving with my right, I begin to spray the windshield. The wiper broke loose from the ice and began to open a small space on the windshield. Now I could see the snow-covered road.

There were so many cars blocking the road that you could not drive in a straight line. I would drive as far as possible on the street and then detour through parking lots, sidewalks, front yards, and any other space that my VW bug could go. After about an hour of spraying and driving, I arrived at James Robertson Parkway and the bridge crossing the Cumberland River.

Again, my logic was flawed. My assumption was the bridge would be heavily salted and free of ice. Wrong! Pulling the car onto the bridge, I tried to gain speed going downhill, which would help get me over the next hill. Logically, it was a sound premise.

There was no salt on the bridge; it was a sheet of ice. Starting down the slope my right hand on the steering wheel and my left still pushing the button on my can of deicer, I increased the accelerator for more speed. Seeing the Cumberland River, the Nashville skyline and the sides of the Memorial Bridge spread out before you like a continuing panoramic motion picture was an experience I will long remember. My VW bug had turned into a spinning top. Thank goodness, no one else was on the bridge. After what seemed like a thousand revolutions, the little VW came to rest next to the curb on the bridge. Straight ahead of me, looking through the snowy rails on the bridge, I could see over a hundred feet directly below me the icy-cold Cumberland River.

I would like to say that I remained calm and cool much like James Bond in his movies, but this was not so. I was shaking like a leaf and not from the cold weather. I was really frightened and, like most people, became more frightened after the crisis was over. Sitting there for a few minutes, I regained my composure. After reassessing the situation, checking my pants, and finding that no accidents had occurred in that area, I checked the car. Thankfully, there were no damages. Surprise. Surprise. My spray can of deicer was still in my left hand. I started my faithful VW, eased back out on the icy bridge, and from that point on, the drive home was an exemplary lesson in extreme icy-road driving safety. The driver education instructor would have been proud.

Arriving home, cold and exhausted, the television was reporting school buses stranded all over the county. Businesses took students inside to warm them and wait for a way home. The school buses were not moving; in fact, nothing was moving. The city had come to a complete stop. Some students did not get home until the wee hours of the morning. This snowstorm came through Nashville at the most inopportune time and actually stymied movement throughout the city. It was one for the record books.

A GUN AND THE GAME

Cohn High School had a winning football season. Everyone was surprised and elated since it was the first winning football season in several years. I always found it strange, but very consistent, that when a school had a good football season, everyone's attitude is better, and the year is more successful and productive.

The basketball team, unlike the football team, struggled early in the season but steadily improved. At the start of our basketball season, I went to the gym to watch the team's practice. After watching practice for a couple of days, I did not see much hope for the teams, especially the girls' team.

I asked Coach Pope, the girls' coach, in a jokingly manner, "Do you want to call the season off before it starts?"

He laughed and said, "Give us a little time. These girls are hard workers and will improve."

I smiled and said, "Going to hold you to that."

A few weeks later, the basketball teams were doing much better than I had anticipated. All our athletic and social activities had been uneventful. Regardless of our good start at all school events, I employed several police officers and, when available, a female officer.

We were playing our rival, and the gymnasium was almost full, our largest crowd. Four officers were on site, three male and one female. The female officer was a slender tall African American. She was one of those individuals that did not walk. She glided, which made her very graceful and enchanting. Her fluid movements were those of an athlete. Once you spoke with her, it was obvious that she was serious about her work. I was told she had played professional basketball. It would have been interesting to talk with her about her pro basketball experience and why she came to Nashville, but I always made it a point not to distract the officers at school events.

Everything was going smoothly until a teacher came to me and said, "We have a problem with a former student, and I think he has been drinking."

Somehow, he had purchased a ticket without anyone smelling the alcohol. He probably had the bottle hidden in his coat and drank it in the restroom. Another teacher had him cornered in the lobby of the gymnasium. The individual was slender, about five feet seven inches tall with a scraggly wannabe beard, attempting to cover his face. When I arrived, he was becoming unruly and loudly using profanity. His reoccurring statement was "You, damn bastards, can't make me leave! I got my rights, and I got my ticket."

Trying to keep the situation from escalating, I calmly said to him, "You can't stay here. You've been drinking."

He got close to my face with a breath that would rival an outdoor privy in the middle of July and said, "You ain't making me go nowhere. You, you, stupid son of a bitch."

I shouldn't have done it, but his comments combined with his breath were more than I could take. I grabbed him by the collar, jerked him around, and drug him down several steps to the outside door. By this time, he was trying to resist and made a couple of drunken swings at me. I pushed the panic bar to open the door, threw him outside, slammed, and locked it behind him.

I hesitated for a minute, looking through the window to make sure that he was not injured from the fall he had taken. He slowly got up and started staggering toward a parked car. I headed back to the ball game. Just as I entered the gym, I couldn't believe what I saw.

The clock was running, and players were in the middle of the court, along with the entire crowd from the left side of the bleachers. The officials were blowing their whistles and waving their arms. I thought, *What the heck is happening?*

Trying to grasp what was transpiring, I scanned the gym for answers. Many of the adults on the gym floor were pointing to the empty bleachers they had just exited. I looked to my left, and midway up the bleachers, the female police officer was talking to a lady.

After a few seconds, the lady handed the officer her purse. With the purse in hand, she escorted the lady down the bleachers and outside the building. I was not sure what was going on and was not going to interfere since it appeared that the policewoman had things well in hand. After they left the building, the officials directed the spectators back to their seats, and the game continued.

After things calmed down and the game resumed, I went outside to talk with the lady officer. By the time I got to her, she was helping the handcuffed spectator into a patrol car.

As the car drove away, I asked, "What happened?"

"In the middle of the crowd, that woman pulled a gun from her purse and threatened her boyfriend."

It was obvious the officer was a little shaken. She was about to explain the details to me when the student that I had earlier thrown out of the game came up behind her. Apparently, he had fortified himself with more liquid courage and began tapping the officer on the shoulder and saying, "I got my goddamn rights, ain't no son of a bitching bastard going to keep me out of the game."

He picked the wrong person to pester this time. She turned around without a word, slipped a flat blackjack from her back pocket, and smacked him on the left side of his head. I had seen it in movies, but this was the first time I saw this action in real time. The young man did not say a word, look around, or move; he just collapsed and wilted right in front of my eyes. The officer turned around and continued our conservation as if this blackjacking was an everyday occurrence. The young man was lying behind her in a crumpled position and obviously unconscious.

The officer continued, "I sent that woman downtown, charged her for disorderly conduct and carrying a concealed weapon."

I replied, "I appreciate your professionalism and quick action. You handled a dangerous situation and probably saved lives."

She looked at me eye to eye and slightly nodded her head affirmatively.

We entered the gymnasium together, and there were just a few seconds left in the game. As spectators begin to leave the gymnasium, my supercop moved to the edge of the basketball floor to gain a good view of the crowd's movements.

After the fans left, I made my way over to the lady officer and said, "I want to thank you again and tell you how much we appreciate you."

Once again, she nodded and then followed the crowd toward the exit.

Checking outside, I found very few people milling around. I guess the gun incident encouraged everyone to find a safer place. The only action I saw was an officer helping *I-got-my-rights drunk* into a squad car. I was glad this game was over.

Early the next day, the Tennessee Secondary School Athletic Association (TSSAA) executive director, Gill Gideon, called and said, "Mack, what happened at the ball game last night? The officials did not wait until the next day to file their report. They called me right after the game."

"Mr. Gideon, it was scary there for a while. We had a domestic situation that involved a firearm," I replied.

"Yeah, the officials reported there was a gun at the game. What did you do?"

"We had a very competent police officer that disarmed the lady, booked her on charges of disorderly conduct and carrying a concealed weapon. Unless she made bail, she's probably still in jail."

"Okay, Mack. Write a report and send it to me. I think you did all that you could do."

I was grateful that the TSSAA did not penalize our school.

That weekend, I was visiting with a friend Joe Crockett, who was a state senator. I told him about the gun situation at the basketball game and was bragging on the lady officer and explaining how her quick action probably kept people from being injured or maybe killed.

Joe took what I said very seriously and said, "We need to stop this kind of behavior. I'll see what I can do about it."

I had forgotten about our conversation until a few weeks later when I noticed in the newspaper that he had sponsored a bill in the

Tennessee legislative body that would make it a felony to bring a firearm on the school grounds. To my knowledge, that law is still active.

The following week, we were having another home basketball game. I asked our athletic business manager to be sure to get in touch with the female officer and retain her for game security.

He returned to my office the next day and said, "Dr. Hargis, I talked with the officer you requested. She said, and I quote, 'There is no way in hell I am going back to Cohn High School.'"

I can't say that I blame her after what she had been through, but she handled a potentially dangerous situation with professional efficiency.

DuPont High School

IMPROVING THE TEST SCORES

Test scores were not an issue in education until the mid to late 1970s when the ACT and SAT college entrance exams began to fall in comparison with previous years. The scores in the United States began to decline while other countries' test scores improved or remained stable. This information caught the attention of political leaders, and fear spread that future generations would not be competitive in the world market. News media and politicians seeking reelection spread this fear. President Ronald Reagan commissioned a national blue ribbon committee to study the problem. After eighteen months, a report was issued known as "A Nation at Risk." The government sprang into action and pursued ways to monitor the academic abilities of graduating high school students and put pressure on educational systems to improve.

One major result was what became known as competency testing. Each graduating senior had to pass a test to receive an academic diploma. Realizing that testing had far-reaching implications—not only for students, but teachers, administrators, and community—we began researching ways to improve our test scores.

As ideas began to surface, the English Department suggested we focus on vocabulary because approximately 60 percent of the American College Testing exam (ACT) and the Scholastic Assessment Test (SAT) tests related to understanding the meaning of words. That theory made sense to me.

This program had to encompass the entire school. Giving each student a list of words and telling them to memorize the meaning would accomplish nothing. Research shows that young persons have to interact with a word meaning approximately twenty-eight times before it becomes an integral part of their vocabulary. We had to develop a procedure that would not add an extra burden to the students or teachers and would inject into the school creative learning interlaced with some humor.

Our plan became known as "Word for the Day." The title was not earth-shockingly creative, but the structure was interestingly different. The first task was to create a list of words that were used in tests, such as the ACT, SAT, and other college materials. This task fell to Mrs. Carol Pettus of the English department. She accomplished her task in short order and developed an exemplary vocabulary list.

Mrs. Pettus stated, "I used words students would use in reading more than conservation and compiled the list from the book, *Vocabulary for the College-Bound Student* by Harold Levine."

The list was double-checked for accuracy, duplicated, and given to each teacher. The printing department developed a desk calendar with the word and meaning, and they were issued to each teacher.

Based on the twenty-eight-time theory, we wanted the word used as many times as possible. Each day, the students making the morning and afternoon announcements would pronounce the word for the day over the intercom, give the definition, and use the word in a sentence. When possible, the word was integrated into the announcements that usually resulted in the word being repeated as many as five times.

Each teacher was requested to write the word on the chalkboard, along with the meaning and a sentence using the word. During class, the teacher would use the word in her lesson as much as possible. If there was a test that week, the five words were integrated into the test. Each student had six classes, which after hearing the morning and afternoon announcements, their exposure to the new word was close to the magic number of twenty-eight.

The *Nashville Banner*, a local newspaper, discovered our program and interviewed a few of the DuPont students.

May King, a junior and third place spelling bee winner, stated in her interview, "It was fun, and we learned a lot."

Sophomore Ty Fodera said, "It has increased my vocabulary. I feel I can carry on a better conservation using these words."

To add a little more student activity and exposure to the words, we organized a spelling bee. The words came from our list and the ACT and SAT test. A committee chaired by English teacher Shirley Maynor developed guidelines for the spelling contest. To make the sometime dull spelling bee a little more exciting, we pitted the classes against one another.

Each teacher conducted a mini spelling bee during the home-room period. After the winners were selected from each of the three classes, a date was set for the school finals. The spelling bee was to be held before the student body. I was not sure how the students would react to watching a spelling bee. To spice things up, we invited a local popular disk jockey (DJ) to be master of ceremonies.

On the day of the spelling bee, the students were dismissed to the gymnasium, seniors first, followed by juniors, and sophomores. After everyone was seated, the DJ started the program with some teenage humor. Even with the humor, the students were somewhat subdued, which concerned me that the assembly could be a big flop.

The rules were double elimination, which insured the program would not end prematurely. Each contestant would have to misspell two words to be eliminated. There were six spellers, two from each grade level. We projected three minutes per word, and that would allow a minimum of thirty minutes for the assembly. All was going well except for the unusual calmness that seemed to be settling over the student body.

As the first few words were spelled without error, there was nothing but the dullness of a day fishing without a bite steadily moving through the gymnasium. Suddenly there was a misspelled word. A senior had faltered. A sophomore was next in line. With renewed interest, a hushed stillness enveloped the entire gymnasium. The student body became so quiet that the public address system was not needed. The DJ pronounced the word, gave the meaning, and asked the tenth grader to spell it. The sophomore hesitated, pronounced the word slowly and deliberately, then began to spell. On the completion of the spelling, he again pronounced the word. The atmosphere of the gymnasium was beginning to tense. The sophomore class—some standing, and others on the edge of their seats—were anxiously awaiting the DJ's decision.

The DJ looked at the speller and with a smile said, "That is correct."

The sophomore class went wild. They were as excited as if attending the finals of the state basketball tournament. After the first explosion of victory from the sophomore class subsided, a few degrading chants came from tenth-grade individuals directed at the seniors. The sophomore class humiliated the senior class with their chants, which opened the door for razzing the opposing class. The crowd's enthusiasm and competitive chants increased as the contestants narrowed. Trophies were awarded at the conclusion of the contest. The spelling bee had successfully exposed the students to the word list once again. My apprehensions were unfounded. It was a good day thanks to the superb planning of the committee.

The winner of the spelling bee, senior Neal Cole stated, "It made learning the words easier."

Sophomore Chris Drumwright, second place winner, commented, "When it is fun, more people will do the extra work."

The most comprehensive student statement concerning the Word for the Day came from Ronnie Gibbs when he said, "It has helped a lot in reading. If you don't know the meaning of one of the words, you can't get the full meaning of the sentence. I have run across a lot of the words we have learned."

The day was encouraging, and everyone walked away with a feeling of satisfaction. I began to think and plan for next year.

Earlier, we had pre-tested the students on the word list and later post tested them. There was a marked improvement in the post-test scores. The program tentatively seemed to be a success. There was no way to know for sure until data could be complied and analyzed. Data would have to be collected over the next few years to determine the degree of success. Unfortunately, this was never to be. The following year, DuPont High School was closed due to the court-ordered desegregation.

GOD WOULD NOT REVEAL
HIS IDENTITY

This particular spring day was like morning glory blooms opening with the beauty of nature, projecting a warm and friendly atmosphere. I drove to work at 5:30 a.m. before most people had ventured out of their homes to pollute and disturb the stillness that Mother Nature had so carefully laid before us. I began to have my all-too-often recurring thought, *Wonder what rapscallion is going to ruin my day?*

As principal of DuPont High School driving to work at 5:30 a.m. seems somewhat ludicrous until one realizes that the powers that be voted to start school at seven o'clock. I understood why they did it even though the decision goes against all research and the natural development of adolescents. The reason was the lack of money, which causes so many ill-made decisions.

Arriving at school, I went to my office and outlined objectives for the day. Nine times out of ten, many of these are never accomplished due to unscheduled day-ruining interruptions. The school buses began to arrive, and I went to meet them. The students came gushing out the bus doors, laughing and talking. Fifteen minutes later, the first bell rang, and students scurried to their classes, and the day began. I strolled through the halls, aiding stragglers who did not want to find their classrooms. This took about thirty minutes, and to my surprise, I found very few needed my help. It just might be a good day. Returning to my office, I began to fill out the unending reports that the state and federal governments require. There were approximately two-hundred-plus reports that had to be completed each year. Two reports were completed, and it was lunchtime. Only two hours to go for a great day.

Finishing an uninterrupted lunch, I returned to my office to attack the next report. Suddenly a teacher, face flushed and visually exasperated, came running into my office, pulling a student by the arm. Sparks of anger were shooting from the pupils of her eyes. The young man in tow seemed to be calm, and his clothes intact, indicating that no physical violence had taken place, at least not to him. He did walk with a limp, but nature had given him that deformity at birth, but not so for the teacher; her dress was torn, she had lost a shoe, and was breathing heavily. Her face was as red as a fox's butt during pokeberry time, which made her bright eyes stand out like blue pools surrounded by molten lava. The bottom hem of her dress was pulled loose, and her right sleeve ripped at the cuff.

I left my state reports, hurried around my desk, grabbed the student's arm, and stepped between them. The teacher was mumbling something about God and some other nonunderstandable words. I waited a few seconds for the teacher to calm down and regain her breath.

She angrily explained, "This student disturbed my class on Shakespeare. He yelled from the hall into my class that he was God. When I caught him, he would not tell me his name."

I told the teacher in my most authoritative voice, "I will take care of this student and will get back to you this afternoon."

After I felt the teacher had regained her composure, I said, "Stop by the office restroom and get yourself together before going back to your class."

I knew the students should not be left unsupervised, but she needed to look in the mirror before returning to class, and I needed badly to get her out of my office before I laughed in her face.

A thorough investigation found that God had left another classroom in the guise of going to the restroom. On the way past the teacher's classroom, he heard her expounding the virtues of Shakespeare and he had a friend in her class.

As her voice was booming about Shakespeare, he slowly bent down to the door air vent and yelled as loudly as he could, "Roger, Roger, Bobbs, this is God speaking. You had better change your ways, my son."

The teacher was so shocked she dropped her textbook and ran to the door. As she opened the door to detain God, the hem of her skirt caught on a rough edge of the door, and the tug made her almost lose her balance. The only thing keeping her from sprawling facedown on the floor was the doorknob. The sudden twist flipped one of her shoes off, causing it to slide across the smooth, freshly waxed terrazzo floor, bouncing from the wall on the opposite side of the hall. The teacher, on one shoeless foot, was agile enough to maintain her balance and continue the pursuit of God.

She called out, "Young man, you better stop."

She managed to overtake God just before he started to disappear down the stairs. God had one leg two inches shorter than the other, slowing him enough that the teacher could apprehend and drag him to the office. She questioned him to no avail as they made their way to my office. God remained silent.

After sifting through the information, it was determined that God was guilty of disturbing the study of Shakespeare. The student (God) was given a punishment equal to the crime. I never found how the teacher tore her sleeve as neither God nor the teacher could remember. The teacher's shoe was retrieved undamaged. I ask the building custodian to repair the rough edge on the door just in case God decided on a second coming.

After everyone left the building, I sat in my chair, looking at unfinished reports on my desk. As I sat sipping a well-deserved coke, the real heavenly God and I had a delightful chuckle.

A VISIT FROM THE SHONEY'S BIG BOY

Shoney's Big Boy Statue

This day was going to be beautiful. In just a few weeks, school would be out, and then the world would be wonderful. I was on my way to work a little before six o'clock. I always arrived early to plan my day and have a few moments of quiet before the onslaught of academically starved students.

DuPont High School is on the eastern outskirts of Davidson County in a community known as Hermitage, located close to President Andrew Jackson's home. Hermitage was a good community, very supportive of the school, and just a good place to live.

Living in Hermitage and going to DuPont was almost like stepping back in time. The students were enjoyable and had a lighthearted mischievousness about them.

This particular morning, I arrived on campus, parked my car, and surveyed the marquee to see if any letters had been rearranged overnight. The school had an entrance porch that was approximately thirty feet long and at least twelve feet wide. As I started toward the door, I looked up and, on the front porch entrance roof, saw standing magnificently in all his glory, a Shoney's Big Boy statue. I took two steps back, rubbed my eyes, and looked again to make sure that what I was seeing was reality. Yes, there he was. Big as life, a Shoney's Big Boy statue on the DuPont High School roof. He looked huge from where I was standing.

There had been some mischief going on last night. Shoney's headquarters was located approximately five miles from DuPont High School. I'm sure some students saw a Shoney's Big Boy statue standing by himself, looking very lonely and appearing to need a home. The students solved his problem. There he stood at home on top of the entrance porch. I will have to say he looked very happy standing there with one hand stuck up in the air, holding his big hamburger. My dad had told me about the old days when kids would take a wagon apart piece by piece and reassemble it on the roof of a farmer's barn. This was something similar, except the Shoney's Big Boy was all in one piece, so no reassembly was required. I begin to wonder, *How the heck did they get him up there?* Then it occurred to me—how am I going to get that fat rascal down?

While I stood staring up at the big boy, my custodian, Mr. Simms, came out the door and said, "Looks like we have a new mascot."

We both chuckled at that remark, and I said, "Do you have a ladder?"

Mr. Simms replied, "Not one that will reach the top of the porch, but there is an entrance to the roof from the boiler room."

"Give me a minute to put my coat in the office, and I want you to show me how to get on the roof."

I looked at my watch, and it was five minutes till six o'clock. We had about thirty minutes to decide what to do with Mr. Big Boy.

Mr. Simms took me into the boiler room, and there in the left corner behind the boiler was a steel ladder attached to the wall, ascending about twenty feet high to a two-by-two-foot-square trapdoor.

"Mr. Simms, when was the last time that trapdoor was used?"

He shrugged his shoulders and said, "I am not sure. Several years."

I hesitated for a minute to scan what other options were available—none! I started up the twenty-foot ladder. As I had reached the top, I saw nestled in the left corner of the trapdoor a four-inch rounded dark object. I stopped my climb and began to search my brain. It's springtime, and the snakes are out. Could this be a snake curled up in the corner of the trapdoor or maybe a wasp nest? Nah, too early in the year for wasp's nest. What the heck could it be?

Not being the extremely brave sort, I backed down the ladder and asked, "Mr. Simms, do you have a flashlight?"

"Oh yeah, right over here."

I took the flashlight and started moving slowly up the ladder. As I got about three quarters the way up the ladder, my mind began to say, *You are close enough. Maybe too darn close.* I stopped climbing, took the light, and shined it at the trapdoor. What I saw was a combination of relief and then panic. Located on the trapdoor were spiderwebs and a large dirt dauber nest stuck next to the door hasp. Hanging from the hasp was a big rusty lock. I knew I could handle the spiderwebs and the dirt dauber nest, but how was I going to get that lock off? I came back down the ladder.

"Mr. Simms, there is a lock on the trapdoor. Do you have a key?"

His reply was "Yes, it's this key hanging on the wall next to the ladder. I completely forgot about the lock."

I thought, *That makes sense. Why didn't I see it?* I took the key, moved rapidly up the ladder, brushed away the spiderwebs, and the mud home of the dirt daubers. Putting the key in the lock, it turned ever so slightly.

"Mr. Simms, the key will barely turn."

Without blinking an eye Mr. Simms said, "Catch this."

He tossed me a small can of penetrating oil. I caught the oil can and heavily doused both the key and the lock cylinder. After pitching the oil can back to Mr. Simms, I inserted the key into the lock. Bingo, the key turned, and the lock popped open. I pulled the hasp down and pushed the trapdoor open. Sunlight shot through the opening like a *Star War's* laser. I climbed through the trapdoor and surveyed the roof. I could see all sorts of things on the roof, mostly athletic equipment. There was a basketball, a couple of baseballs, softballs, tennis balls, baseball bats, and a pair of pink panties. The top of this building was another world. Oh, I almost forgot, and a Shoney's Big Boy.

I called down to Mr. Simms and asked him, "Would you go to the front entrance porch? I will meet you there."

I made my way across the top of the building, avoiding stumbling on the athletic equipment that was scattered about. Making my way to the porch and the Shoney's Big Boy, I was beginning to realize what the students had accomplished. The statue was towering above me by at least a foot. Here I was, on the roof of the entrance porch standing face-to-face, or maybe face-to-stomach, with this giant big boy dressed in his red-checkered trousers, brown mop of hair, and a hamburger in his right hand raised to the sky.

My mind began to churn. *Now, that I'm here, how am I going to get him down?* It was a bigger job than I had anticipated. I was beginning to appreciate the ingenuity of the students that placed him there. I could throw him off the roof, and I really wanted too, but he would break into a thousand pieces.

I called down to Mr. Simms again, "Do you have a rope?"

His reply, "Not one long enough to get that thing down."

I was beginning to semipanic, thinking, *I am not going to get this big boy down before the students arrive.*

Walking over to the edge of the porch and looking down at Mr. Simms, I said, "Is there anything that we can…?"

Then Mr. Simms, and I saw the answer at the same time.

We had recently planted red and white impatient flowers in the front of the school, our school colors. Mr. Simms had been very diligent in watering these flowers. We both saw the hose that he used to water the plants.

Mr. Simms said, "Back up. I will try to throw this hose on the roof."

With that, I heard a grunt and saw the majority of the hose come flying over the edge and smacking Mr. Big Boy right in the middle of his hamburger-fattened gut. I grabbed the hose and tied it under big boy's arms so he would not slip through and turn into a humpty-dumpty. Wrestling this oversized hamburger sign to the edge of the porch and using the hose, I gently lowered him to the ground. When on the ground, Mr. Simms pulled the Shoney's Big Boy under the porch and onto the concrete walk while I climbed down the boiler room ladder. Mr. Simms went into his closet and brought out an appliance dolly that made moving Mr. Big Boy much easier as he was heavy and awkward to handle. We both looked at each other in disgust; there was another problem to solve.

The big boy looked too big to go through our front doors. We rolled him up to the front door, and we were right. He was too darn fat. The school had double door entrances, but there was a latch bar between each double door. The latch bar was the obstacle that was inhibiting our success.

Mr. Simms looked up, smiled, and said, "Hold on."

He reached to his belt and grabbed a large ring of keys. Fiddling through keys, he grabbed an Allen wrench, unscrewed the set screws, and removed the latch bar. That intelligent and quick-thinking solution allowed us to roll the chubby statue through the doors. Once we got him inside the building, we put him into a double door closet and locked it.

"Mr. Simms, thank you for your help."

He smiled and said, "We won this one."

Shortly after we locked Mr. Big Boy in the closet, students began entering the building. We had made it with only minutes to spare. I watched closely to see if any students were staring at the roof or producing any other unusual behavior that might indicate they were one of the pranksters. They were about as cool, concealing their identity as Mr. Simms and I were in disposing of their prank.

We contacted the Shoney's Corporation about their kidnapped big boy, and he was eventually returned to the rightful owners. The DuPont grapevine never produced the names of the guilty parties involved in the Shoney's Big Boy caper. To this day, I still do not know who engineered and carried out this mischievous act. It would be interesting to know how they got the big boy on the roof. The Shoney's Big Boy kidnapping will rank high on my list of all-star school pranks.

I will always be appreciative to Mr. Simms for his help with the Shoney's Big Boy and especially for keeping the school immaculately clean. Mr. Simms was like most everyone that worked at DuPont. They did an outstanding job and never received the recognition they deserved. DuPont High School was an excellent school that was a victim of politics and the federal government.

NEGOTIATING WITH KIDNAPPERS

Keith Dearing Statue-Napper   Paper Mache Statue of Liberty

At DuPont, we had our share of talented teachers. One such teacher was Corrine Wright, who taught history and had more energy than most of her students. Ms. Wright was always looking for a project that was beyond the normal curriculum. I found that if she had a project that would engulf her, things seemed to run smoother for the entire school. She was also very helpful and supportive of school-wide activities, such as the Spelling Bee, Word for the Day, and her own event, "Taste Food From Around the World Night." She was a unique woman and teacher that would stand her ground if she thought she was right.

One of Ms. Wright's projects that is vividly locked in my mind was the day she got involved in raising money to revitalize the Statue of Liberty. The Statue of Liberty in the early 1980s had become in disrepair, and people across the country were asked to donate money for repairs. Ms. Wright immediately took on the task. She and her students built a papier-mâché Statue of Liberty that was the exact color of the aging statue. It was a remarkable job. The statue was about five feet tall and identical in every way to the statue in New York Harbor. She and her students were extremely proud of their accomplishment. In fact, the statue was so good that many businesses in the community requested that she bring the statue to be displayed in their stores. Naturally, she accepted a small donation for the statue's appearance, and this money was sent to the Statue Revitalization Fund. Everything was going well with donations, and appearance requests were coming in daily.

One morning, Ms. Wright came bursting into my office, waving a piece of paper and saying, "Look what they have done! Look what they have done!"

I asked, "What are you talking about?"

She handed me the piece of paper and typed on the paper was a statement, "If you want to see your Statue of Liberty again and in one piece, you must meet our demands."

Sometime during the evening, unsavory characters had slipped into the school and kidnapped the Statue of Liberty. They were negotiating with Ms. Wright for the statues return and were demanding a small sum of money. More importantly, the kidnappers were also demanding decreased homework and the elimination of weekly test. This was very serious. Paper-mâché is not extremely durable, and we did not know how long the statue could withstand the rough treatment of captivity.

Ms. Wright said, "What are we going to do?"

I looked at her for a moment and thought, *These kids have a real imagination. Let's play along with them.*

"Ms. Wright, you have to negotiate with these rascals."

She looked a little surprised and then said, "Okay, I can do that."

As she left the room, I smiled to myself and thought, *This could be interesting.*

After a day or so of negotiating, Ms. Wright came to my office to report things had taken a dark turn. Left on her desk was an envelope with not only the repeat of their original demands but photographs of the most disparaging actions that papier-mâché kidnappers could possibly threaten. The photographs displayed the Statue of Liberty humbly standing with a blindfold tied tightly over her eyes. It was obvious by the photographs that the Statue of Liberty was being threatened and tortured. Not only was she blindfolded, but there also in the photograph were two water pistols pointing at her head. This was very serious; one squirt from the water pistol could melt an ear or cause the nose to droop. Hoping for the safety and the unmutilated return of the statue began to fade. Bravely, Ms. Wright continued to negotiate with the kidnappers throughout the week. Demands and counterdemands were thrown back and forth with very little progress for the return of the statue.

The safety and well-being of the statue was of great concern. Not only was safety an issue, but a more pressing problem was the Statue of Liberty had an engagement Saturday morning in the mall to be displayed at the entrance of a business. The statue had made several engagements prior to the kidnapping, and her popularity was growing. If negotiations failed and she did not appear for her appointment, this would be the first black mark on the statue's social/business calendar. Trained negotiators could not have done a better job than Ms. Wright, but the kidnappers held to their demands.

Negotiations had been going all week with very little progress. The Statue of Liberty's engagement was Saturday morning. We were hoping the statue would reappear on Thursday, but this did not occur. After talking to Ms. Wright, we finally decided to pull out all stops and put heavyweight pressure on the kidnappers.

My policy on school announcements was to always have students make them. Very seldom did I speak on the intercom, but when I did, I felt the students paid closer attention as this was a change from the norm.

Thursday, following the afternoon announcements, I took the microphone and explained, "The Statue of Liberty has been missing for quite some time. She has an engagement Saturday at the mall, and we do not want to disappoint the business that requested her appearance. It would be in the best interest of all concerned if Ms. Liberty were returned undamaged to her rightful owner. No questions will be asked."

The next morning, Ms. Wright came joyfully into my office and said, "The statue is back and unharmed."

With that information and a smile, she left my office. The statue made her business engagement and several others as the year progressed. I never found out who the inventive, mischievous kidnappers were until thirty-three years later.

I went to a high school basketball game to watch a friend's daughter play.

While sitting in the bleachers, a stout tall young man walked up to me and said, "Dr. Hargis?"

When I first looked up, I did not recognize him. Then suddenly everything clicked. He was a student at DuPont High School when I was principal. His name was Keith Dearing, and he was a darn good basketball player. He sat down, and we talked for a while about former students and the DuPont days. Then the Statue of Liberty crossed my mind, and I asked Keith if he knew anything about the Statue of Liberty kidnapping caper.

He looked at me with a sheepish grin on his face and said, "Yeah, I know all about it."

Keith explained the original intent for the kidnapping was to raise money for the Statue Revitalization Fund. As negotiations continued, new ideas kept popping into their heads, such as reduced homework, weekly test, and water guns. We laughed, and I told him I thought it was ingenious and added a little spice to the school year. DuPont High School was full of good, mischievous, fun-loving, intelligent students.

HELP FROM THE OLD FOLKS

Mayor Richard Fulton and the Retiree Tutors

In 1983, politicians in the state of Tennessee, as well as the entire nation, were using education as a whipping post to enhance their political ambitions. According to most local politicians and news media, the Nashville schools were deplorable. In their eyes, the only way to improve the schools was to develop guidelines for graduation and mandate a curriculum. To ensure the students were ready to meet the world and receive a diploma, they were required to pass a test. The special needs students who would be challenged to pass were required to take the same test.

My first year at DuPont High School was the state's first attempt at diploma testing. The senior students were given a practice competency test to see how many would pass and to check the validity of the test. The following year, the test was given, and it was not practice. We had done several things to encourage the students, such as banners in the hall, motivating announcements, and class competition spelling bees held with the entire student body watching. We did well on the test but really wanted to do better. All these activities were good, but we were not isolating the students who really needed help.

One day, shortly after lunch, my assistant principal, Mr. Hugh Price, came into my office and said, "Mack, I'd like you to take a look at what I found in this educational journal. The school they discussed in this magazine used retirees to tutor students. According to the article, this was a very successful program."

As he explained the details, I became intrigued. We would have to make some adjustments to the program to fit our needs, but it just might work.

I asked Mr. Price, "Do you think we should give it a try? It'll take some planning and teacher cooperation."

Mr. Price replied, "It sure can't hurt anything,"

The next day, we set aside time to preorganize the program and determine if it were a possibility. After outlining the basic program, we discussed it with the guidance counselors, and they agreed to do the extra work for a feasibility study.

A retirement village was located just a short distance from the school. Our first step was to ask retirees at McKendree Manor if they would be interested in helping with our tutoring program. Neither Mr. Price nor I knew any retirees at the home, nor did we know any of the management. It was going to be a cold call. We were keeping our fingers crossed. The following day, we scheduled an appointment with Mr. Reagan, McKendree Manor's director.

After school on the day of the appointment, we met with Mr. Reagan at his office. We spent thirty minutes outlining our proposed program. After we finished, we sat in silence for what felt like forever and a day. Finally, after a short deliberation, his response was "I don't know if we should do this. You know how dangerous the schools are, and these residents are my responsibility."

"Mr. Reagan, schools are not nearly as bad as the news media portrays them. You haven't seen DuPont in the news, have you?"

"No, I don't think DuPont has been in the news lately."

After a short hesitation and a thoughtful glance around the room, he said, "I'll tell you what we can do. We will let the retirees make the decision. I will tell them about it and see what they say."

Mr. Price and I thanked Mr. Reagan for giving us this opportunity. We shook hands and started out the door.

Mr. Reagan said, "Just a minute, I want you to know that I am not going to put any pressure on my folks to come to this meeting. I will announce it, and that's all."

"We would not want you to put any pressure on them," I replied. "If they don't want to be involved with the program, it would not work anyway."

A week later, Mr. Reagan contacted us that the meeting was scheduled for three o'clock Wednesday afternoon. That was perfect. School would be out, and we would have plenty of time to meet with the retirees.

On the day of the meeting, Mr. Price and I were apprehensive not knowing what to expect. Mr. Reagan met us at the door and escorted us through the lobby that was furnished with beautiful sofas and chairs all focusing on the large screen fold-out television. McKendree seemed be a very pleasant place to live. As we rounded the corner, Mr. Reagan motioned us to an area about the size of a school classroom with tables, chairs, and many activities to keep a person from succumbing to boredom.

In the room, there were six individuals sitting quietly, waiting for us. After Mr. Reagan's introduction, he turned the meeting over to us. I opened by briefly explaining the new state policy that required all seniors to pass a competency test in order to graduate. The retirees asked a few questions concerning the test and then remained silent.

I explained, "I appreciate you being here, and we need your help. We have a few students that have trouble grasping academic subject matter because they learn a little slower than most students."

The climate in the room was still slightly tense, reminding me of the silence in Mr. Reagan's office the week before. Then a gentleman in the back row broke the tension when he said, "Yeah, I understand that. I was one of the slow fellows."

Everyone laughed as one person commented, "Yeah, right. I thought so."

And another, "You still are."

After the ice was broken, Mr. Price and I began to field questions from the retirees. And as we both expected, there were comments concerning safety and how terrible the schools were. We both knew that we could not tell them how great things were at DuPont and make them believe it.

I looked at them, thought for a minute, and said, "Why don't y'all come to the school and have lunch with us? We will show you the school, and you can see the students. If you will accept our invitation, we will provide transportation, and lunch is on us."

The invitation stirred a little uneasiness among the retirees. They turned and looked at one another, not knowing what to say. I had put them on the spot. I realized that the program was going to live or die on their decision.

Then again from the back row, the same gentleman in a commanding voice said, "I don't think we should turn down a free lunch."

Everyone laughed, and we set the date for the visit.

Mr. Price got their names and told them we would come for them at eleven o'clock. The first hurdle had been cleared. They were going to enter the school.

On the day the retirees were to have lunch with us, we informed the student body and staff that we were having guests for lunch but did not reveal the reason for the visit.

When we arrived at McKendree, the retirees were all dressed with their Sunday go-to-meeting clothes. They looked sharp. Everybody but my buddy from the back row—he was in khakis and a sports shirt. He looked good, but not in his Sunday best. Mr. Price and I escorted the retirees into the cafeteria and showed them where to sit.

I asked them, "Would you like us to serve you lunch or do you want go through the lunch line?"

They looked at one another, and a petite lady with silver hair said, "Let's go through the line."

I said, "Great. Come this way."

All the while, the students were watching the guests, and the guests were keeping a keen eye on the movements of the students. The misgivings that the retirees expressed had not left their minds. After the retirees sat down to enjoy their lunch, Mr. Price and I left them alone to experience DuPont High School and feel free to talk among themselves.

We stood at the edge of the cafeteria and observed the students and retirees. A few of the students stopped by and talked with the retirees. This was not planned, but I was not surprised given the caliber of the students that attended DuPont. After lunch and between class changes, we gave our guests a tour of the building. During the tour, there were a few questions, but mostly, a low tone conversation among the retirees. I was not sure what their conversation would mean for our tutoring project.

On the short drive back to McKendree Manor, there was very little conversation. I was dreading this question, but it had to be asked.

Arriving at McKendree Manor, I said, "Well, what do you think?"

After a brief hesitation, the petite silver-haired lady and my back-row buddy exchanged glances, and he replied, "We need a little time to think this over. We will ask Mr. Reagan to call you," as the other members nodded their heads in agreement.

"We will expect his call, and we enjoyed having you," I replied.

While everything had gone better than planned, there was still a question in my mind, *Will this project ever get a chance?*

On Wednesday of the following week, Mr. Reagan called and said, "The group enjoyed visiting DuPont and are interested but have some questions. Could you meet with them tomorrow?"

"Sure, what time?"

"About the same time as the last meeting, three o'clock."

Mr. Price and I had no idea what the retirees wanted to discuss, but just the fact that we were meeting with them was considered positive. At three o'clock sharp, we entered the building and went directly to the activity room. The retirees were already assembled and waiting for us. To our surprise, there were ten people in the room.

I said, "Hello, we understand you have a few questions for us."

The silver-haired spokesperson said in a pleasantly sounding, soft voice, "Yes, we do, and a few other people have heard about the program and may also be interested."

My anxiety started to fade as I thought, *We can make this work*.

After welcoming the new attendees, I opened the floor for questions. The retirees' questions were intelligent and well thought out. They wanted to know things such as the following: What their responsibilities were? What were the guidelines of the program? How they would get to DuPont?

When we got to the last question about transportation, I thought we might have an unsolvable problem. We had been in the process of trying to obtain transportation for the program, but everyone that we approached had a conflict and could not help. I was trying to think on my feet for an appropriate answer when a familiar voice spoke up from the back row.

Once again, my back-row buddy saved the day. He said in his deep, commanding voice, "Aw, don't worry, girls. I got wheels."

Everyone laughed, and the problem was solved. The ball was in our court now. We had to get into an organization and implementation mode.

While Mr. Price and I had been working with McKendree Manor, our guidance department had been assimilating the names of students who were in danger of not passing the competency test. The test was divided into subject areas, which allowed us to pinpoint the student's weakness and set up a tutoring program for that individual. After we determined the at-risk students, the guidance counselors discussed this program with them to determine if they had an interest in being tutored. All the students wanted to be involved in the program. A meeting was scheduled to introduce the students to their tutors.

We had to schedule the tutoring sessions during the school day as some students rode buses and could not stay after school. Innovative scheduling developed by the guidance department allowed a student weak in English and strong in math to meet his English tutor during his math class. A tutoring session was never scheduled during the class of a student's weak subject. The month before the tests were given, each at-risk student was scheduled for two tutoring sessions a week. If the tutor and the student wanted extra sessions, arrangements would be made.

After the first week, everything worked smoothly. The guidance counselors did an excellent job coordinating the student and tutor's study sessions. I was relieved that no problems developed between the students and the tutors. In fact, many of the students and senior adults developed a grandparent-type relationship. The tutors took their job seriously, and some came by and asked if they could have a place to do extra work after school with their student. Those requests told me that if this program were not successful, the cause would not be the lack of interest and dedication.

As the date for the exam approached, the students and tutors were putting in even more time preparing. Finally, the day arrived, and the students walked into the room with a newfound sense of confidence, ready to face off with the test.

It always took several weeks to receive the test results. While waiting for the test scores, an interesting phenomenon took place.

Students would stop by my office and the guidance office, inquiring, "Have the test scores come in yet?"

Not only were the students coming by to check for the test results, but the tutors were also calling and asking about the status of the test scores. A bond had developed between many of these senior adults and the students.

For me, one heartwarming situation developed when the scores did finally arrive. A student stopped by the office and said, "Dr. Hargis, have you told Mrs. Daniel that I passed the test?"

I replied, "No, not yet. We were going to call the tutors this afternoon."

A broad smile came across his face as he said, "Good, please don't call her. I want to tell her myself."

As he turned to leave, I said, "Good idea. She will appreciate that," while a warm inner glow covered me and an almost tear crept to the corner of my eye.

This program's success went beyond our wildest dreams. DuPont was honored by Nashville Mayor Richard Fulton with an award for innovative programs in schools. The *Nashville Banner* did a story on our program and interviewed several of the tutors.

The *Nashville Banner* related that the tutoring program not only benefited the students but also the senior adults as reflected by Mrs. Daniel, a retired attorney's comment, "I wanted to do more than sit around and play Rook. I thought older people have something to contribute, and we do. So I said I will help the boys and girls."

Ms. Frances Faulkner, a Hume-Fogg High School retired teacher, stated, "I have more faith in public education now."

Mr. Thomas Wade, a teacher of forty-six years, said, "Most of the students were just scared of the test. I enjoyed helping them."

I think it is important to note that two students who passed the test were in special education. I have often wondered if any other school had accomplished this feat of *all* students receiving an academic diploma. It proved to me, without a doubt, that any child can learn if they are given the attention they deserve and have a desire to learn.

Bobby Brown, DuPont guidance counselor, summed up the pride and success of the program when he stated to the *Nashville Banner*, "DuPont was the only school in the Metro Nashville school system to have 100 percent of its seniors pass their proficiency test,"

The sad part is that DuPont High School was closed the following year due to political and judicial decisions related to the integration of the Metro Nashville school system. To my knowledge, the individuals at McKendree Manor were never again asked to participate in a tutoring program. They did an excellent job and, I am sure, changed some students' lives.

I personally will be forever grateful to them.

The Youth Banner

Nashville, Tennessee □ Wednesday afternoon, June 6, 1984. □ Music City Media □ 4 pages □ Youth edition

Students make the grade
'Word-for-the-day' success at Dupont

By Jane Srygley
Youth Banner Editor

Dupont High School students had fun this year learning new words.

It all began about three months ago when Dupont principal, Dr. Mack Hargis, read in an educational journal that a large portion of all intelligence tests, such as SAT, ACT and PSAT, are based on a person's vocabulary knowledge. He and the faculty started to think about how the school could help students increase their vocabularies, and they came up with the idea of a "word-for-the-day."

Through the combined efforts of the school's English, business and printing departments, they developed a word-for-the-day calendar. Included on the desk calendar is the word, its definition and its use in a sentence.

English teacher Carol Pettus selected the words from the book *Vocabulary for the College-Bound Student* by Harold Levine. "I tried to pick words they would use in reading more than in conversation," she said, "and I used the book for college-bound students because I wanted the words to be challenging, even to the good student."

Ms. Pettus came up with a list of 51 words, ranging from the fairly common "rationalize" and "dogmatic" to the more difficult "labyrinthine" and "bacchanalian."

Before the school began its word-for-the-day, the students were given a written test on the words. The tests were graded by the Metro Board of Education's data processing department. Seven percent of the 712 students taking the test made 65, a passing score.

For the next three months, following the moment of silence each school day, the students were given a word-for-the-day. Hargis said the words also were used in the morning and lunch announcements, which are broadcast to the student body everyday.

Later the faculty came up with the idea of a school spelling bee on the words. Teacher Shirley

Maynor chaired the committee which drew up the rules for the spelling bee. Each homeroom chose a speller who competed for the grade championship. Then the grade champions competed for the school champion.

At the end of the school year the students took the same vocabulary test they had taken three months ago. There was a marked difference in scores — 50 percent of the students scored 65. "The scores were even better than I had anticipated," said Hargis, who plans to continue the word-for-a-day concept next year.

Although students are required to learn vocabulary lists in English classes, the word-for-the-day concept was described by Hargis as "casual learning." In other words, he said it wasn't a pressure-type of learning; their goal was to make it fun to learn.

"It was fun, and we learned a lot," said junior Mae King, third-place winner in the school spelling bee.

Senior Neal Cole, who won the school spelling bee, agreed. "It made learning the words easier," he said.

"When it's fun, more people will do the extra work," added sophomore Chris Drumwright, second-place winner in the spelling bee.

Earning extra credit and playing games with the words added to the learning process for senior Joy Fitzpatrick. "We could earn extra credit, and we played games with the words, such as we would see who could make up the most sentences using one of the words," she said.

Now the students are reaping the benefits of their new knowledge. "It has helped a lot in reading," said junior Ronnie Gibbs. "If you don't know the meaning of one of the words, you can't get the full meaning of the sentence. I've run across a lot of the words we've learned."

"It's increased my vocabulary," said sophomore Ty Fodera. "I feel like I can carry on a better conversation using the words."

Neal said he likes using the words in writing. "I like to be able to use a word more precise in meaning," he said.

23

Friday
March
1984

dogmatic (dog mat' ik)

asserting opinions as
if they were facts;
opinionated; asserted
without proof

Drawing by David Lawrence

See how good your vocabulary skills are

Dupont High School students showed a marked improvement in their vocabulary skills after participating in the "word-for-the-day" program.

Below are some of the words they learned during the three-month project. Do you know the definitions?

1. eclectic
   a. choosing from various sources
   b. never seeming to grow old; ageless
   c. assumed or simulated to impress others
   d. open to the air; breezy
2. indubitable
   a. certain; incontrovertible; indisputable
   b. good-natured; agreeable
   c. of or involving walking
   d. overbearingly proud; haughty
3. plausible

TRY THIS

a. characterized by savagery or coarseness;
b. without the usual or appropriate cover
c. showing or possessing excellence or bliss
d. superficially true or reasonable; apparently trustworthy
4. laconic
   a. intended as punishment
   b. using words sparingly; terse; concise
   c. amusing; humorous; pertaining to comedy
   d. close and firmly united or packed
5. lethargic
   a. disobedient; mischievous
   b. expressing negation, refusal or denial

c. neither masculine or feminine in gender
d. unnaturally drowsy; sluggish; dull
6. bucolic
   a. of or pertaining to country life
   b. bending in and out; winding; serpentine
   c. arousing pity or sympathy
   d. capable of bearing affliction with calmness
7. propinquity
   a. a speculative or risky undertaking
   b. kinship; nearness of place; proximity
   c. rapidity or speed
   d. the leading position in a trend or movement
8. contiguous
   a. inspiring hope
   b. touching; near; adjoining
   c. feeling or showing hostility

d. having all parts; whole
9. abstemious
   a. sparing in eating and drinking; temperate
   b. immoral or unchaste
   c. cautious; on one's guard
   d. not dense or crowded
10. pristine
    a. in original, long-ago state; uncorrupted
    b. secluded from the sight, presence, or intrusion of others
    c. finicky, fussy and prudish
    d. enormous; extraordinary; marvelous
11. arbitrary
    a. successful; victorious
    b. afflicted with woe; mournful
    c. proceeding from a whim or fancy; capricious
    d. universal; world-wide

Answers: 1 a, 2 a, 3 d, 4 b, 5 d, 6 b, 7 b, 8 b, 9 a, 10 a, 11 c.

Nashville Banner Article

AFTER-HOURS CONFLICT

The night was dark; no moon in the sky, and the temperature was extremely warm for the first Friday in November. It was 11:15 p.m. DuPont's last football game of the year was over, and the season had been mediocre at best. Being principal, I was grateful and was looking forward to a few Friday nights at home before basketball season.

Following my after-game pattern of stopping by the local drive-in market for a snack, I found my normal parking spot occupied by a slick red Prelude. (The warm weather brought out the locals in mass.) The parking lot was crowded. The market was located a few hundred feet from the Cumberland River. A large trailer park on the banks of the river kept a steady flow of customers to the market.

The trailer park's community was diverse with both black and white living in quiet, fragile harmony. A few people owned their trailer, but most rented and were members of the city's lower socioeconomic group. Most individuals in the park were busy trying to earn enough money to make ends meet and did not have the time or energy to fight over the color of a person's skin.

As I entered the market, Alf, the owner, threw up his hand and said, "Hey, Mack, did you win tonight?"

My reply was "Nah, but it is over for this year."

"Guess that's something to be thankful for. Want your usual warm Honey Bun?"

"Yeah, that Honey Bun would hit the spot. I need a little comfort food."

"What do you want to drink with this bun? Coffee? I just brewed a fresh pot."

"Naw, it's too hot. Think chocolate milk would taste good."

The first bite of the warm honeybun dripping with sugar sent a smooth, comforting feeling though my tired body. The cold milk washing the bun down was the pinnacle of a late-night snack.

After wiping my mouth, I said, "Seems like a lot of people out tonight."

Alf looked around and replied, "This snap of warm weather has brought them out of every crack around here, especially the young ones. They ought to be home in bed, but the parents don't care, so they run wild."

"Noticed a few kids milling around when I parked my car."

"Did you see the cop car down the street?"

"No, didn't pay any attention. Just too tired, I guess."

"You know they stop in here every night for a free cup of coffee, which I am glad to give them. They always offer to pay, but I won't take it. It's good to have the officers around here. Keeps problems down."

"Makes sense. That's why we have them at the games. Having any problems tonight?"

"No, not yet. A lot of kids around, but so far, so good."

Just as I started to leave, a daytime employee that Alf had hired, in hopes the young man could get his life in order, came through the door. He was six feet, two inches tall and somewhat of a want-to-be bully. He bought some cigarettes without saying a word and seemed to be preoccupied.

The shot of honeybun sugar combined with the cool milk sent my energy level up several notches. I stood at the window, watching teens scurrying around the parking lot while savoring my new surge of sugar power.

Alf interrupted my thoughts by saying, "See anything interesting out there?"

His question disturbed my sugar-energy surge and brought me back to reality.

"No, not much. I just realized my car is the oldest and most pitiful in the parking lot."

"Yeah," Alf said. "Those kids probably owe more on their cars than you do on your house."

"Yeah, probably. It's getting late. Guess, it is time to go home. See you later, Alf."

"Right, later," he replied.

The parking lot was a crowded mess, and rather than trying to negotiate through the teenagers, I decided to drive the back way by the loading dock. The market lights in the back were dim but ample for low-level night vision. As I rounded the corner by the loading dock, there appeared to be some commotion in the field behind the market. My car lights had not been turned on, and the individuals were not aware of my presence.

Stopping the car, I watched what was taking place. Five or six teenagers had formed a circle, and two individuals were in the center. The two in the center seemed to be dancing with one another. They were an odd couple. One was tall, head and shoulders above his partner. They moved around the ring, ducking and bobbing, and the smaller of the two would occasionally make dashes to the edge of the circle, only to be roughly pushed back.

Getting out of my car, I slowly moved closer and hid in the shadow to get a better view. The tall person in the middle of the circle appeared to be Alf's employee. The shorter and faster individual I did not recognize in the dim light.

While trying to process this strange ritual, a car turned into the market. Briefly flashing light on the group, revealing the smaller individual in the circle was a young black boy who looked to be twelve-or-so years old. As he ran to the edge of the circle, the circle members would grab and hit him, forcing him back to the center toward Alf's employee. Realizing what was happening really ticked me off. There was no way this small black kid could have provoked all these white thugs.

Without thinking, I stepped from the shadows and said, "What is going on here?"

They all froze with startled looks on their faces. Normally, I take my tie off after the ball games, but this time, it remained around my neck. Seeing a white shirt and tie stepping from the shadows loudly barking orders was a shock to them.

My next volley was "There's a cop car across the street. Y'all want to be arrested?"

All the white kids suddenly disappeared in a cloud of dust. The only person left was the small black boy. He was slowly moving toward me. About twenty feet from me, he stopped, bent over, and started fumbling with something on the ground.

Walking to him, I asked, "Are you okay?"

When he looked up, I could see he was not okay. His lip was bleeding, and he had a cut above his left eye. He said, "I'm all right" while bending over to pick up a torn paper bag of groceries.

I said, "My car is over here. I'll take you home."

We picked up the spilled items and put them in the torn sack, and I pointed to my car without saying a word.

Sitting in the car under the dome light, I could see his wounds much better.

I took a tissue, cleaned his face, and asked, "Where do you live?"

He pointed toward the trailer park and said, "Down there."

He directed me to his house by pointing and said not a word. When we arrived at his house, the torn grocery bag caught my attention. It was wet down one side.

"Did something break in the bag? Do we need to go back to the market?"

He flashed a surprised look and said, "Nope."

When we stopped beside his home, I asked, "Do you want me to come in, talk to your parents, and explain what happened?"

Slamming the car door, he said, "No!" and disappeared into the green-and-white trailer.

I slowly made my way out of the trailer park, wondering, *Why do these things happen? It's just does not make sense.*

HILLWOOD COMPREHENSIVE HIGH SCHOOL

THE HILLWOOD CLUMPS

I was transferred to Hillwood High School after DuPont High School was phased out due to the federal desegregation court order. Hillwood was located in the more affluent area of Nashville; Belle Meade had the reputation of where the superrich of Nashville lived, and Hillwood was adjacent to Belle Meade. The Hillwood Country Club was located next to the high school. On a warm day from the school parking lot, one could see country club members tee up their golf balls.

     H. G. Hill, a wealthy businessman, who made his fortunate from grocery stores and real estate, donated the land for the Hillwood High School campus. He was a civic and ecologically minded person.

I had been told by several people that Mr. Hill had put in the land gift agreement several conditions and requirements that must be followed if the Nashville school board was to maintain control of the property.

One of those conditions was that no chemical control agents were to be used on the grounds or in the building. This put an extra burden on the grounds crews, maintaining the large fifty-two-acre campus. Due to the lack of chemical aid, there were several areas on the campus that were overgrown with weeds and small brush.

The overgrown areas were the first improvement that I wanted to accomplish at Hillwood. A very important item of my personal educational philosophy was to make the physical building and surroundings as inviting as possible. There was much work to do on this campus. I called the school system maintenance department and ask them for help.

"We have a lot of thickets and overgrown places that need to be cleaned up. When can you do it?"

"Dr. Hargis, you can send in a requisition for your request, but to be honest with you, we are shorthanded, and that type of request will not be a high priority."

"In other words, you are telling me that the brush will not be cleared by your department."

"That is about the size of it."

I didn't like his tone or what he said. I closed the door to my office, took off my coat, and changed into my work clothes. I had purchased some mums on the way to school to plant in front of the school marquee. After planting them, I backed off to admire my handy work.

Not bad. Not bad at all, I thought. The marquee was green, and now the bottom border was outlined by yellow mums. I knew matching colors was not my best talent, so I hoped it looked good. While dressed in work clothes, I decided to take a closer look at the wilderness clumps scattered across the back acres of the campus. As I walked to the first group of bushes, I could see blackberry, honeysuckle vines, and small scrub trees growing around a pile of rocks.

Going to each clump, I found myself at the back entrance to the school. The entrance was used mostly by vocational students.

As I turned to survey the amount of work to be done on the campus, I was overwhelmed. My first thought was for a group of students to help me with the work, but that was not possible. The job was too big, and if we managed to cut the brush, how would we depose of it?

While pondering what to do with the weed clumps, my thoughts were interrupted by screeching tires. A black Mercedes was sliding sideways, barely missing a Ford Mustang that was leaving the auto mechanic department. Apparently, the student was attempting to get on the street and check out his work on the car.

A loud "Watch what you are doing! You almost killed me! Pulling out in front of me like that!" followed the tire screams.

"I'm sorry," said the young man, sitting in the car that was almost in the ditch. "I did not see you. I am so sorry."

The large black Mercedes was sitting crossways in the road with an irate older man at the wheel, wearing an expensive suit and red power tie. As he moved toward the Ford, his face and eyes were beginning to match his tie.

He said to the kid in the car, "Are you all right? There is no damaged done this time, but you need to watch where you are going. We could have been killed."

The young man apologized again and said, "I did not see you. Those bushes and the sun blinded me."

There was no response from the older man. He wheeled around in a huff and left the almost-accident scene. When he accelerated, I could hear his tires bark as he sped down the road.

Not to be outdone, the student in the little red shiny Ford squealed his tires and threw gravel over the street.

I walked to the tire squeal scene and observed the black marks on the pavement. It appeared the little Ford had left a couple of hundred miles of rubber burned into the asphalt. I looked up and down the street from the position of the little Ford. The kid in the red car was correct; the bushes were obstructing the view of the oncoming traffic.

That blind spot was another potential safety problem, along with the weeds and bush. Those clumps could be the home of all kinds of snakes and other unsavory varmints, as well as student's hiding places.

This job was too big and could not be accomplished by a community cleanup day. Contract work would be too expensive. No help from the maintenance department on a large job such as this left me somewhat perplexed. I was beginning to understand why the former principal had not tackled the problem.

That weekend, I talked to a friend, Joe Crockett, a state senator. I described my problem and said, "This area needs to be cleaned up, but I can't get any help from the school board."

"Do you want me to call the school board and put some pressure on them? Is that why you are telling me? I will call them if you want me too."

"No, no, I don't want you to call anybody. Just venting a little to clear the mind."

"Why don't you call the sheriff? They do public service work like that. You know the sheriff. You met him at his campaign rally last year."

"That is a great idea. I remember him. Hope he remembers me. Thanks a lot. I'll call him Monday morning."

I called the sheriff, and he remembered me, or at least said he did. He told me who was responsible for public service projects and transferred me to that office.

The project supervisor said, "Let me check our schedule. Let's see…huh…yeah, we can be there on Tuesday morning of next week."

"Thank you. We will have everything ready, and don't bring lunch. It's on us."

The day the sheriff's inmate crew was to arrive, we had everything ready: several cases of soft drinks, individual bags of chips, sandwiches from the cafeteria, and candy bars from the vending machine.

The crew arrived at nine o'clock and attacked the weed clumps with a vengeance. By lunchtime, they had cleared most the weeds and had started loading the debris on trucks. It was eleven thirty, and the foreman asked us to bring lunch. I grabbed a case of cold drinks and headed toward the workers.

Suddenly I heard someone loudly calling my name, "Dr. Hargis! Dr. Hargis! Over here! Over here!"

My first thought was that one of the inmates had heard the foreman use my name and was calling me to bring his group the first serving of soft drinks. I kept on my path and did not turn around.

Then again, only louder, "Dr. Hargis! Dr. Hargis! Over here! Over here!" was the cry.

I delivered the case of drinks and then looked in the direction of the voice. Again, he said, "Over here."

I walked toward an almost-cleared weed area and saw a young man, skinny and well-tanned. He had a wild mop of hair that made him look like a fugitive from a teen werewolf movie. As he stepped toward me, his face became familiar. He smiled a wide toothy grin and said, "Do you remember me? I was at McGavock, and you were my principal. You were right. You told me if I did not change my attitude, I would wind up in jail."

"Yeah, I remember you, Jerry. This is one time I am not happy about being right."

He smiled again, white teeth shining brightly against his tanned face, and said, "Don't worry about it. You tried your best. Maybe I will straighten up someday."

I handed him a coke and said, "I hope so, and you were a pretty good body and fender man the best I remember."

Jerry smiled again, seemly glad I remembered him, and nodded. He took his lunch and returned to his work crew.

The brush was almost gone. Only cleaning the campus of small limbs remained. The crew chief estimated about an hour more. I ask the foreman if he could send a couple of men over to trim the bushes that almost caused an accident a few days ago.

His reply was "Sure, those three will go with you."

We walked to the entrance of the vocational parking lot. I instructed the crew what bushes to cut. About the time they were really making progress and cut bushes were flying in all directions, I heard a loud gruff voice. "What do you think you are doing?"

There was an older silver-haired man wearing white Nike warm-up pants with a pink stripe down each leg. His shirt was pastel pink with a polo logo on the breast pocket. His large feet were sporting white Nike tennis shoes. Wearing white tennis shoes, pants, and a pink top made him look like a giant aging Easter Bunny.

I replied, "We are trimming these bushes."

He said, "You can't do that! It's in my deed that there will be a buffer between my property and the school."

The crew had stopped cutting the bushes and were watching our interaction. I motioned for them to continue trimming the bushes. I was not about to lose this free labor. This dangerous intersection needed clearing.

I crossed the road and said, "The bushes have to be trimmed to improve the vision for the cars. We almost had an accident here a few days ago."

My speech accomplished nothing. His nostrils were beginning to flare, and his face was flushed as his breathing rapidly increased.

"If you don't stop, I will get an injunction and make you stop."

"If you force me to stop and an accident happens, you could be held responsible" was my rebuttal.

I slowly moved back, just out of arms reach, and said, "We are cutting the bushes that obstruct the view of the intersection. It is a safety issue."

He snorted, "I will not—"

I interrupted him saying, "We are only cutting the bushes around the intersection, but if you want us to cut more, we can accommodate you."

"No, no, don't cut anymore. That is enough!" he shouted as he began to shuffle back to his house.

I was glad he left. I could see the headlines in the morning paper: Hillwood Principal Provokes Attack from Older Man over a Bush Dispute. That would be a great start for a new principal.

My crew completed the trim work and headed back to the main body of workers.

The foreman said, "It is time for us to load up. I think we got everything done. If you need us again, just call."

I thanked him profusely and threw a couple of cases of soft drinks and chips on the truck. As they drove away, my former student and I exchanged waves, and I wished him well. I turned to view a neat, clumpless campus. They did an excellent job.

The results were pleasing, and I had a lot of people to thank for the good job, especially the sheriff and Senator Joe Crockett. The first problem was solved.

Racial Fight at Hillwood

Hillwood had several busloads of inner city students from an area known as Dodge City. This was a tough area of Nashville. Hillwood also had the unfortunate legacy of a student losing his life during the school day. This death had resulted from a scuffle over a yearbook. One student pushed the other, and as he fell, his head hit a steel door.

The Hillwood complex was a conglomerate of three different buildings. The vocational building was located between the high school and the elementary building. It was a hodgepodge maze and poorly designed for navigation. One particular point of congestion was the exit from the high school building to the vocational building. The only way to go from the high school building to the vocational department and vice versa was to negotiate your way through one set of double doors. A large number of students had to use this entrance at every class change. The bottleneck inhibited traffic flow. This particular area often caused tempers to flair and invited fights to erupt.

Another situation that invited disruption and sometime resulted in fights was when students were not under direct supervision, such as changing of classes, in the lunchroom, and assembly programs, such as pep rallies. To alleviate some unsupervised areas, teachers were asked to stand at their doorway during class changes, and the lunchroom was staffed with monitors. When going to and from assembly programs, there was less supervision as both teachers and students were moving.

I had been principal of Hillwood for approximately one month. Our first football game was Friday night, and a pep rally had been scheduled for the activity period. I was apprehensive there might be trouble during the pep assemble. But to my pleasant surprise, the rally went off without a hitch. The captain of the cheerleaders thanked the students for their participation and told them to report to the third-period class. As the students exited the gymnasium, I moved into the hall for observation purposes. Everything had gone so well. I returned to my office.

Just as I entered the office, a teacher rounded the corner and said, "Dr. Hargis, Dr. Hargis, there's been a fight!"

I turned and took two quick steps toward her and asked, "Where is the fight?"

"At the vocational doors. It's over now. We know who they are."

The teacher gave me their names, and I asked the secretary to retrieve their class schedule cards.

Mrs. Cox, my secretary, said, "Do you want me to send for them?"

I replied, "No, I will get three of them, and Mr. Gunn, my assistant principal, will get the other two."

When I arrived at the classrooms and asked for the students by name, the class was hushed and not a person spoke, not even the teacher. The students got up from their desk and came with me.

I ushered the three students to my office. The assistant principal was waiting for me with his two fighters. Seeing that the fight had been between black and white students irritated me but did not surprise me as Hillwood was known for having racial problems in the past.

Normally, assistant principals handle the discipline cases. The students had been at school for two weeks, and the first interracial fight had taken place, and everyone was watching this new principal. I knew my actions would set the racial disciplinary climate for the year.

I told the black students to go into my office and kept the white students in the outer office to prevent another fight.

I turned to the assistant principals and said, "Thank you for bringing them to the office. I will handle this."

Mr. Bill Gunn said, "I know these kids. I'll be glad to take care the problem."

Mr. Dennis Crowder, another assistant, repeated, "Yes, we can deal with these kids."

My reply, a little more firmly this time, was "I'll handle this problem."

I appreciated their willingness to help, but I wanted to set the tone for this type of behavior.

I directed the two white students to follow me into my office. Closing the door, I sat the two white boys between the black students. Sitting behind my desk, I did not say a word for a few minutes and just looked at each kid across the desk from me.

Then I asked one question, "What happened?"

That's when they all started talking at once and pointing fingers and using profanity.

I watched and tried to listen for about five seconds and said, "I cannot hear nor understand everyone talking at once. The only thing I clearly hear is the profanity, and that is to stop. We are going to speak one at a time, and no one will interrupt while that person is speaking."

We started on the left side and moved to the right, giving each person an opportunity to share his opinion. As everyone had his turn to speak, it became obvious that the speaker was not guilty; the others were at fault. Also, the white students and black students were teaming up against one another as they spoke.

After listening to the group for approximately thirty minutes, I could see that no progress was going to be made as each group blamed the other. It was easy to see the fight was racially motivated. Their words emanated distrust, and hate flashed in their eyes as they talked. After the last person spoke, I asked if anyone wanted to add anything. There was no reply.

I looked at each student and said, "Fellows, we are not going to put up with this kind of behavior at Hillwood. After listening to your comments, it does not appear that any of you are interested in an education and are only interested in causing trouble. I'm not going to let you disrupt the school for students who do want to get an education."

It appeared that neither their attitude nor facial expression had changed or was going to change. My next statement did change their facial expressions.

I said, "I do not want to see any of you at this school again. When you get up and leave this office, don't come back. If I see you on school grounds, I will have you arrested. Do you understand me?"

Three black students had an expression on their face of surprise and disbelief. One white student was looking at me and shaking his head no, like this can't be happening. The larger white student still had that sullen, I-don't-give-a-damn look on his face.

I said, "Get up and get out of here, and don't come back!"

The students filed out of my office into the entrance foyer of the school. I was watching them from my office door to monitor their actions. They stayed in the foyer for approximately ten minutes, walking around, shaking their heads, and expressing in body language, *What am I going to do?*

After watching them for that short time, I walked to the foyer and instructed the boys to come closer so I could speak with them.

I said, "If any of you really want to come back to school and behave yourself, this is what you must do."

Suddenly the group became very quiet and started listening intently.

"You must tell your parents what has happened. If they will come back to school with you and meet with me, we might let you back in school. Do all of you understand you do not come back to the school without your parents?"

Interestingly enough, four out of five of the students said, "Yes, sir."

I did not really expect to see the parents for a few days if at all. But I was pleasantly surprised. This fight took place on Friday, and Monday morning, I had three of the five parents waiting to see me at 6:45 a.m., two black parents and one white. All conferences were successful. The parents were cooperative and understood. Students were sent to class following the parent conference.

On Tuesday morning, another black parent came to school and talked with me. We reenrolled her son. The only student that did not bring his parents was the larger white student. I never heard from him or his parents, and my phone calls were not returned. He was eighteen years old, in the tenth grade, and could legally quit school without any complications.

We had few racially motivated fights the remainder of the year. I often thought dealing with the first racial fight firmly and fairly had a positive impact on the school year. Of course, you could never know for sure.

THE ROACH DEN

Anytime you move into a new position, there are unforeseen situations that emerge. Even though you have been warned about them, they can still be a surprise. A problem that I had been told about but had not personally seen was roaches. The imposed chemical band gave the roaches a slight advantage. As the year progressed, I would see a roach or two scurrying across the hall, trying to escape the onslaught of students' shoes during class change. Occasionally, one would venture into my office early in the morning or late at night after a ball game. These roaches did not seem to be ordinary school roaches. I had encountered vermin in other schools, but Hillwood's had their own special characteristics.

Most of the roaches were large, about two inches long and three-quarter-inch wide. Their back was a hard brownish shell that resembled a battle shield. If one were brave enough to corner these monsters, you might encounter their secret weapon. They could fly! It was bad enough to attempt stomping one of those speedy rascals, but when they took flight, all you could do was frail the air, hoping to keep them off your face. They were fast enough that I considered putting them on the track team.

As my encounters became more frequent, especially during cold weather, I decided to do battle with the brown-winged scourge. One night, after a basketball game, I went to the cafeteria for a pot to store some items leftover from the hospitality room. When I turned the light on, the floor came alive. Everything moved. I switched on more lights for a better view, looked again, and they were gone. The floor had been covered, and suddenly, they were gone! Where did they go? I got the pot, washed it, and took it to the hospitality room.

Monday morning, I talked with the cafeteria manager and asked, "When you open in the morning, do you see roaches on the floor?"

She replied, "I see a few on the floor, and they disappear as soon as I walk into the room."

"Then you don't see the roaches as a real problem?"

"Oh yes, in a food prep area, one roach, I consider a problem."

"What is done about it?" I said, putting her on the spot.

"Well, they come out once a month and spray, but what they use does not do much good. We wash the pots and pans before we use them and keep all our food in the cooler and in airtight containers," she explained.

"I guess that is about all you can do," I replied.

The roaches were not causing an outward problem, and most Hillwood people had become adjusted to an occasional bug running across the floor. I kept wondering, *Where do they go*? I looked under tables, behind trash cans, in closets, and could find maybe one or two.

Where do they go? kept running through my mind.

One Saturday, I was at school completing a useless state report. After about an hour, I decided to give my back a short rest by walking the halls. Almost immediately, my back began to feel better. I rounded a darken corner and saw several roaches in the middle of the hall. There was one larger roach in front of the group of smaller, less threatening insects. They did not see me for a few seconds. It appeared they were going through some type of intensive training. As soon as they saw me, they rapidly disappeared into a crack in the floor made by an ill-fitting trapdoor. I had not noticed the trapdoor before. I tried to open the door, but it was securely stuck. Trying to open it with every tool I had—knife, letter opener, a screwdriver, and a fork—nothing worked. Returning to the office, I made myself finish the report. Driving home, I kept wondering what was beneath that trapdoor.

I arrived early Monday morning and tracked down the custodian. He was busy unlocking doors by taking chains off the panic bars. Most of the panic door locks were worn badly, and without the chains, a short jerk on the handle would open the door.

"Mr. Searcy," I called, "do you know what is under the trapdoor in the hall by the library?"

I startled him because he is usually alone in the early morning. After regaining his composure, he replied, "You mean the one over to the side of the hall?"

"Yeah, that's the one. What is under there?"

"That is a tunnel. It is only three feet deep, and it goes throughout the building."

"Okay, and what is in it, and what is it for?"

Mr. Searcy grinned and said, "That is for all the wires and pipes that feed the entire school. There are several of those doors throughout the building. I have been here at Hillwood for eighteen years, and I have seen the maintenance department open the doors only a few times."

"How do you get the doors open?" I inquired.

Again, a smile, then said, "You take a crowbar and stand on the side of the trapdoor closest to the wall. This will cause the other side to slightly rise. Take the crowbar and slide it under the raised side. Then come around to the other side of the door and pry it up."

"That sounds simple enough. Was it designed that way to keep students out?"

"No, over the years, I found I could get the door open by that method. I open it once a year for inspection."

"I appreciate the information. I was just wondering what the doors were for."

Now I know where the roaches go. The next question, what to do about it?

The next weekend found me at the school following Mr. Searcy's directions using the crowbar that I brought from home. I stood on the side of the trapdoor, and the far edge of the door popped up. Sliding the crowbar under the popped-up door, I pried it up. As the door opened, I could see a mass of pipes and conduit full of wires. The floor seemed to be slowly quivering as if it were alive. When I shined my three-cell flashlight into the hole, the quivering stopped and turned into a full-scale romp. Roaches were going everywhere, especially further down the tunnel. I leaned over and shined the light down the tunnel. The roaches had evacuated my area, which allowed me a closer look. The concrete floor was covered in a coat of dust and bug droppings. There was a half pack of old Pall Mall cigarettes and a lighter that must have slipped out of a worker's pocket. I guess the roaches were smarter than we humans because the tobacco had not been touched. No telling how long the Pall Mall had been there. Closing the top to that nasty hole, I took my crowbar and headed to the office.

As I entered the outer office, a big brown-crusted roach cut in front of me. The roach then suddenly stopped and turned toward me as if in an attack position. He was not going to run. It was him or me. I moved to the left, and he countered with the same move. He could fly, and I did not want to battle a flight attack. Moving slowly back to my right and then with a quick fake back to my left, I spun sideways and came down hard with my shoe. I knew I had scored a direct hit as I could hear the unmistakable crunch of the brown-winged Hillwood roach. The battle was over as quickly as it started.

Lifting my shoe, I observed the mashed yellow sticky fluid mingled with brown shell wings. Before cleaning the remains from my shoe and the floor, I scanned the room for reinforcements. I saw none. The roach was alone; the battle was similar, I guess, to David and Goliath. Only this time, Goliath won.

After the exhausting battle, I sat behind my desk, wondering how this situation could be improved. Taking a napkin, I double cleaned my shoe weapon and headed for my truck. *What to do? What to do?* kept churning my mind.

A couple of weeks passed without any solution. The school did not outwardly appear to have a problem as the roaches were well trained in staying out of sight.

Schools are inundated with all kinds of magazines and catalogs. My favorite was called *Useful Technology*. It had all the latest gadgets that were made to save the world. As I thumbed through the pages, an item caught my attention. It was an electronic roach chaser called RID-A-ROACH that would produce a high-pitched sound that humans could barely hear but would drive roaches insane. It was guaranteed to rid the premises of all roach-type insects. I had found the solution. Each RID-A-ROACH plugged into an electrical receptacle and would cover one room. The cost for each RID-A-ROACH was seventy-nine dollars and ninety-five cents. Mentally calculating seventy-nine dollars and ninety-five cents times the number of rooms, I quickly realized the school could not afford a full-scale experimental battle against the roach army.

I ask Mrs. Cox to order a RID-A-ROACH.

She looked at the catalog and asked, "Do you think it will work?"

"I don't know. We will find out."

"We can't afford one for every room. That would cost, let's see about—"

I interrupted her, "Order one."

In a few weeks, I received my own personal RID-A-ROACH and immediately plugged it into the electrical wall socket in my office. I could tell right away it was high-level technology. Red and green lights began to flash, and it emanated a faint, irritating buzz. For the next three days, I did not see a roach in my office. This thing just might work.

It appeared to work during this short test, but even if it killed or ran off every roach in the office, we couldn't afford a RID-A-ROACH for every room in the school. My devilishly innovative mind kept saying, *What to do? What to do?* It was Friday, and due to thinking about roach control, I had barely heard the last of the afternoon announcements. The student who was in charge of making them left school in such a hurry that she sat the microphone too close to the internal transmitter that caused a low humming feedback.

I went to rearranged the microphone and to stop the humming. Starting out of the room, an idea hit me and gave me a euphoric felling like I had stepped on the last roach. I thought, *This may work.*

I returned to school early on Saturday morning to try my idea. No one knew about my roach experiment. I was hoping the roaches would not know what hit them. I took my roach killer from my office and plugged it into an electric outlet in the announcement room. The red and green lights were flashing with the low, high-pitched squeal emanating from the RID-A-ROACH. I thought, *It's working perfectly.*

I took the microphone and taped the transmitting lever down so there would be a constant transmission to the entire school. The next task was to lean the microphone against to the RID-A-ROACH. My hope was that it would project the anti-roach sound into the microphone and transmit throughout the building. I left the office and went into an adjacent room. *Yes!* I could hear the low-volume, high-pitched squeal from the speaker.

I patted myself on the back by saying out loud, "It works, and we are going to be roach free!"

Driving home allowed me to think and develop a deep, warm feeling caused by the thought of potential roach annihilation. My entire weekend was very pleasant as the thought of roach killing gave me much joy. I'm sure it was the same feeling as Duke of Wellington experienced as he defeated Napoleon.

Arriving at school early Monday morning, I went directly into the announcement room, untapped the microphone-transmitting lever, and set it in its proper place. The RID-A-ROACH was still flashing green and red as I unplugged it and returned it to my office.

I was in the outer office, waiting for the morning announcements while privately self-glowing on my success. It was time for the announcements. *Where is that kid? Is she absent? Did no one get her a substitute?*

There was some quizzical movement and hushed conversation coming from the announcement room.

Finally, my secretary said, "Dr. Hargis the public address [PA] system won't work."

I went to check the PA, turned a knob or two, and punched a few buttons. My limited electrical expertise could not produce one peep from that machine. The maintenance department was called to repair it. They always respond quickly if a PA system is not functioning.

Maintenance men were at the school within the hour. It is a safety issue. If you have an emergency and cannot communicate with the student body, it could result in disaster. The maintenance man's name was Mike, which seemed appropriate for a person working on equipment with microphones.

After repairing the PA system, Mike was shaking his head as he packed up his tools to leave the building. I expressed our appreciation to him as we walked to his truck.

He looked up and said, "It's strange, really strange. I have never had this to happen before."

I replied, "What do you mean?"

He held a burned clump of metal in his hand and said, "The transformer for the transmitter was burned to a crisp. I don't know what caused it. There was no danger of a fire as it is low voltage and enclosed in metal, but still, very unusual."

My comment, with a straight face, was "Well, you know it is an old PA system."

NATIONAL HOLEY JEANS CONTROVERSY

The day was April 24, 1987, a Friday, and I was anxiously waiting for the weekend. It had been a rough week.

This era was popular for politicians and even comedians to talk and brag about growing up in a very poor environment. This attitude had drifted into young people's psyche. One way, young people identified with this prevailing trend was in their choice of clothing. It became very popular to wear clothes that were tattered and threadbare. The clothing industry made clothes with predesigned holes and sold them for a high price.

My week had been filled with talking to teachers and students concerning class disruptions caused by carefully placed holes in jeans. I counseled with these students and sent a few repeat offenders' home to change clothes. Those who had no transportation home were sent to in-school suspension, a disciplinary study hall, for the remainder of the day. Rather than problems decreasing, they seemed to be accelerating. It was 1:30 p.m., thirty minutes before school was to be dismissed, and the third teacher of that day was leaving my office after complaining about class interruptions caused by students' attire. My last nerve had just been stepped on which resulted in an ill-fated administrative decision.

On the afternoon announcements, I explained, "Students, clothes with holes in them will no longer be allowed at Hillwood High School. This type of clothing has caused entirely too many class interruptions. If you want to wear holey jeans, do so on the weekends. As of Monday, this dress code will become effective. Have a good weekend."

After the announcement, I had a few teachers come by to say, "Thank you." Interestingly enough, the teachers who came by were not the ones that were complaining about class disturbances. At any rate, the week was over, and I had a weekend to relax and recharge my batteries.

Saturday afternoon, I received a phone call from a *Nashville Tennessean* reporter, Amy Gutman, asking, "Could you give some details about the no-holes clothes policy at Hillwood?"

I explained to Ms. Gutman, "The holes in the jeans were causing problems in the classroom. A few of these jeans were bordering on indecency."

Ms. Gutman said, "Thank you," and terminated our conversation.

I thought it was a little strange for a reporter from the *Nashville Tennessean* to be contacting me on a Saturday about a dress code. I dismissed the call by thinking maybe I would get some positive support from the news media.

Sunday morning, my general routine was to rise about 5:00 a.m., read the newspaper with a hot cup of coffee, and enjoy the quiet before my kids and wife woke. I would scan the headlines for any information concerning education, then move to the sports section, and finally, the real estate section. This particular morning, I opened the paper, and on the front page, I saw a picture of three Hillwood students sitting in front of the school with legs crossed, and their knees poking through the large holes in their jeans. In large bold print just below the picture was the headline, *Holey Jeans Controversial at Hillwood.* I could not believe that holey jeans rated the front page of the Sunday newspaper. My next action after reading the headline was to get out of my chair and walk across the room and pick up the newspaper from where I had thrown it.

It must have been a very slow news day, or it was just another opportunity for the news media to take a shot at the educational system as was the trend at this time. Ms. Gutman had been a busy reporter, covering all her bases by calling other schools and assistants superintendents. The schools' replies to her questions were positive to semi-positive on my behalf.

McGavock High School's principal Howard Baltimore stated, "Students would probably not be sent home unless they were causing a disturbance."

Mr. Stanfield, Overton's principal, said, "The student would be sent home to change clothes if half their knee was hanging out."

Glencliff's assistant principal, Nancy Dill, said, "Students who came to school dressed inappropriately would be sent home to change clothes."

After reading the article, I sat sipping my coffee trying to analyze the situation and determine why this article was written. Internally, I was seething. The ringing of the telephone interrupted my pondering. I glanced at the clock, and it was 7:15 a.m.

I thought, *It's starting already. A phone call this early in the morning.*

I cautiously said, "Hello."

"Is this the principal of Hillwood High School?"

"Yes, ma'am. This is the principal of Hillwood High School speaking."

"I am Mattie Agee. I am eighty-three years old, and I just read the article about holey jeans in the newspaper."

She hesitated for a breath just long enough for me to think, *I am going to be raked over the coals about holey jeans at seven thirty on Sunday morning by an old woman.*

After getting her breath, she said, "I am calling to tell you to hang in there, honey. You are right. Sorry to call you so early, but I wanted you to know you have my support."

I said, "Ms. Agee, thank you so much. I just read the article myself, and I really appreciate your call and support. What you just said means a lot to me. Thank you again."

Sometimes unseen powers send you a supportive message at what seems to be your lowest moment. Ms. Agee's call was a boost that I needed.

At church, I also received some lighthearted supportive comments. The remainder of my day was spent answering the phone and wondering what Monday morning was going to hold for me.

Monday morning started about 4:30 a.m. when I forced myself out of the sleepless bed. Completing my preparation for work, my mind continued to wonder what would be in store for me. Knowing the front-page students, I was sure their activity would be well planned and in an area that would produce the most attention.

Normally, I was at school by 6:00 a.m. This morning, I chose to arrive at 6:50 a.m. Classes started at 7:00 a.m., and I knew most students would be in, or near, their first-period class. Whatever was planned for me would have fewer spectators. I stepped from my truck and walked toward the school. The last yellow school bus was leaving, and a few students were dashing to the door, trying to beat the tardy bell.

The outside of the school looked normal with no signs or posters hanging from the building. Entering the door, I saw their plan in all its glory. It appeared I had stepped back in time with the protesting flower-child hippies. There in the foyer sitting on the green-gray tile floor were four boys wearing the worst tattered jeans I had seen thus far this year. Each had their legs crossed Indian style similar to the picture in the *Tennessean*. The knife work on their jeans was extensive. Each student was boldly and definitely poking their lily-white knees through the holes in their jeans.

A few students were lurking at a safe distance, waiting to see what was about to transpire. The protesting students were sitting in the path to my office. I did not stop when I came through the door. As I neared the sitting students, I stepped between them as if they were not there and headed into the office. Not a word nor eye contact was made with the sitters. As I stepped between them, I felt my briefcase slide along one of their heads. Just before I entered the office, I saw from the corner of my eye the onlooking students were dissipating and moving toward their classes.

Entering the outer office, I found it stone-cold quiet. The two secretaries were at their desk but seemed to be frozen in time. The assistant principal was nowhere to be seen. Passing both of the secretaries, I did not acknowledge them, and they treated me the same. The student office workers were huddled next to the teachers' mailboxes, trying to look busy.

I set my briefcase on the desk and noticed next to the phone a pile of messages. Friday evening, the message box was empty. It appeared the secretaries had been busy this morning. That pile of messages would consume most of my day.

Arranging my desk for the day, I glanced through the message slips by the phone. The majority of the messages were from parents, concerning the dress code issue. I asked my secretary to give me a list of the teachers who had first-period planning. From the list, five teachers were selected and asked to come to the office.

The first bell rang, and using the public address system, I asked the teachers to close their doors and admit no one after the tardy bell; this allowed students five minutes to get to their classes. By the time the announcements were completed, the teachers that had been sent for were in my office. I assigned each teacher a section of the building to patrol and make sure all students were in their classes. Any students found in the hall were to be escorted to my office. This patrolling action took approximately ten minutes, and to my delight, there were only three students found in the hall, and none of them were dressed in holey, protesting clothes.

The office was quiet, waiting to see what was going to happen. Teachers did an excellent and efficient job patrolling the halls. Apprehended tardy students were dealt with and sent to class. Teachers were asked to remain in the office for the next few minutes in case help was needed.

Going back to the public address system, I said, "Teachers, I apologize for interrupting your class this morning, but would you please send to the office the names of any students in your class that are wearing holey jeans? Thank you."

In approximately ten minutes, the teachers had sent to me a list of students. Again, to my pleasant surprise, the list of holey jean protesters had only six names out of over thirteen hundred students. Scanning the list of names, I turned to the teachers that helped patrol the halls and said, "Thank you for your help. Everyone did an excellent job, and your work is very much appreciated. I will personally go to classes and bring these students to the office."

The teachers filed out of the office some, saying, "Glad we could help," but most were just glad to get out of the office.

I took the list of holey-jean students and proceeded to their classrooms. Approaching each classroom, knocking on the door, and then without teacher acknowledgement, I entered the classroom. Without saying a word, I scanned the classroom for the guilty. Locating the students that were improperly dressed, and still without speaking, I motioned for them to come with me. There was complete silence in the room. As we left the room, I turned to the teacher and said, "I apologize for interrupting your class. Hopefully, this will not happen again."

The students followed me to my office, and we sat down to discuss this problem. I was hoping to reason with the students and get them back in class as soon as possible. Looking at each student individually, my comment was "I am going to give each of you an opportunity to give a good reason why I should not send you home for ten days."

A stillness fell over the group along with slight shuffling movements from their chairs. After a short silence, I said, "We are going left to the right and give each of you a chance to speak."

The comments were "You can't tell me how to dress, and you are violating my civil rights."

After listening to the students, it was my turn to try reasoning with this unreasonable group. My focus was on parents and their dress while on the job.

"How do your parents dress when they leave to go to work? Do they dress sloppily?" was the start of my rationalizing.

Before I could get a reply from any of the students, I explained, "Your parents go to work each day to earn a living for them and especially for you. In that context, your job is to come to school and be as successful as possible, not only for your future benefit but to please your parents. This includes presenting yourself in a decent manner."

After a brief silence, one student said, "I am going to be a musician, and musicians dress anyway they want."

I replied, "Yes, some musicians dress rather sloppily. You are not a famous musician yet. When you become a famous musician, you can dress anyway you like. But until that time, you are a student at Hillwood, and you will comply with the dress code. Always remember, your actions are a direct reflection on your parents, whether you like it or not."

None of the other students had any comments. Surveying each student's face and movements, it was obvious that this revolt was not progressing as planned. I conjured up my most serious facial expression and said, "Fellows, we have a problem here, and there are several options for consideration. The first option is a ten-day suspension from school, which could impact your grades because you cannot make up schoolwork or tests when on suspension."

All these students were academically gifted and valued their grade point average. It was obvious from the facial expressions that option number one was not acceptable. This option would only be used if their actions went well beyond the present sit-in, but they did not know this.

"Option two is for you fellows to go home, change clothes, and come back to school."

When this option was put on the table, the students began to turn and look at one another, searching for a nonverbal group approval.

Before they could reply, I added a condition to option two. "You, fellows, know that your parents must be notified when you leave school grounds."

This caused another wave of uneasiness. Then I asked them to move to the outer office for a few minutes to give them time to digest what had just taken place. No sooner than the protestors sat down, the student office workers huddled around like bees to flowers, probing for information. I knew the results of our meeting would spread through the school at the speed of light. Also, that no student wants the school to call their parents. The parent calling would be a deterrent to other students joining the "holey" cause.

After ten minutes, each student was asked into my office. Without group support and alone with me in the office, each student reacted differently, especially when I started dialing the phone to contact their parents.

One student said, "Dr. Hargis, you don't have to call my parents."

I looked up, continued dialing, and replied, "Why do you say that?"

The student explained as if he had a discovered alchemist's secret for changing lead into gold. "I don't have to leave the school grounds! I have an extra set of clothes in my car."

That comment brought an inward smile, and his actions reminded me of the beginning of the women's liberation movement ten years earlier when the high school girls would leave home with their bras in place. As soon as they got to school, their first stop was to the restroom for bra removal.

"I think I need to call your parents anyway" was my reply, which did not provoke a positive response from my protestor.

"Aw, please don't call" was the begging reply.

By this time, I had his mother on the phone. "Mrs. Haley, this is Mack Hargis, principal of Hillwood High School, and I have your son in my office. He was involved in a little sit-in this morning and is wearing jeans that are rather ragged."

Before I could complete another sentence, her comments were loud and clear as she exclaimed, "He what! He left home properly dressed. Can I talk to him?"

"Yes, ma'am. Here he is."

I was not privy to their conversation, but it was short with a few "Yes, Mamas, and I will, I will."

He handed the phone back to me, and his mother said, "I am sorry for the trouble he has caused, and it will not happen again."

"Mrs. Haley, thank you for your help and support. Roger is a good student and a fine young man. He just got led in the wrong direction.

"Thank you for saying that. When I get him home, we are going to thoroughly discuss this. Thank you again."

As each student came into my office and phone calls were made, the results were all basically the same. The parents were understanding and supportive with one exception.

When I called this particular parent, he requested a conference to discuss the situation and said, "My son will dress as he wants!"

My reply was "I am sorry you feel that way. I will be glad to talk with you, but until we reach a satisfactory agreement, I am going to ask you to keep your son home."

His disgruntled reply was "That does not seem appropriate. In a court of law, the defendant is not sentenced until he has had the trial."

I immediately realized I was going to be in for an intellectual discussion on the ills of our society. I said, "Yes, sir, you are correct about the courts. This is a high school with over thirteen hundred individuals, not a courtroom. I will be glad to discuss the matter with you at your convenience, but you must keep your son home until we reach an agreement. When do you want to make the appointment?"

His reply was "I will be there at seven tomorrow morning!"

"I will see you then."

The remainder of the day was spent returning phone calls from mostly positive individuals who read the article in the Sunday paper. The article had been sent throughout the country by news networks. This resulted in phone calls and letters from Florida, Arizona, New York, and other states. Several radio stations called for interviews.

My secretary cracked my office door and said, "There is a radio news announcer on the phone, and he would like to interview you about the holey jeans. Are you interested?"

"No, not really" was my reply, "but I guess I had better, so they will stop calling."

Returning from her desk, she said, "He will call back in fifteen minutes."

"Okay, let me know when he calls," I replied.

The fifteen minutes turned into five, and suddenly, I was on the phone with New York City.

The reporter began with "We are on the phone with the principal of Hillwood High School in Nashville, Tennesssseeeee, who has banned the students from wearing jeans with holes in them. Can you tell us what the problem is at Hillwood High School?"

I started with "You are well aware that every school must maintain an educationally sound environment. Any disruptions to this environment must be eliminated."

The reporter interrupted me with another question, which told me he had limited time to devote to this subject.

"Dr. Hargis, what type of disruptions are we talking about?"

I said, "Some students have strategically placed holes in the jeans that boarders on indecency. We thi—"

Again, I was interrupted as he said, "Thank you, Mr. Principal, WKPL listeners, you are the first to hear the *whole story*! Stay tuned for more interesting news events."

His last statement indicated that the entire interview had been set up so he could use his cute little pun. After being the brunt of the New York joke, I decided not be cannon fodder for any other news media interviews.

The day was over, and I had survived. Making my way home in heavy traffic, my little brown and tan Dodge Dakota truck was actually driving itself. My hands were on the steering wheel, eyes on the road, but my mind was revisiting the events of the day as if viewing a sixteen-millimeter film.

I was functioning well, I thought, until an eighteen-wheeler trucker leaned out of his window and harshly brought me back to reality.

"You stupid SOB, watch where you are going!"

Traffic had slowed to approximately ten miles per hour, which allowed me, as well as everyone around, to hear the trucker's chastisement.

My first thought, *He's not going to talk to me like that.*

Two things changed my mind: Number one, he was right; I was wrong. Number two, he was as big as a mountain. I waved in acknowledgement, turned off my mental projector, and concentrated on the task at hand.

I arrived at home safely. Dinner was on the table, and my two girls were eating and talking about their day's activities. Apparently, my holey jeans issue was not a concern at their school. For the remainder of the evening, my Hillwood stress factor was not mentioned.

Tuesday morning began after very little sleep the night before. Two sleepless nights in a row was beginning to take its toll. I went to my truck with coffee in one hand and briefcase in the other. My car keys were in my coat pocket, so I placed my briefcase on top of the truck topper. Fishing out my truck keys, I unlocked the door, put my coffee in the cup holder, started the truck, and drove out the driveway. As I made a right turn onto the street, I heard a loud noise.

It sounded as if a football player with cleats was running across the truck topper. I immediately slammed on the brakes.

The sudden stop reversed the sound from the topper to the cab roof and down the windshield of the Dakota. My briefcase came sliding past the front windshield, over the hood, and down to the road. Fortunately, no one in the neighborhood went to work this early, so I escaped the embarrassment. I rescued my now-scarred briefcase and drove toward my seven o'clock holey-jean parent conference.

I arrived at school at six fifteen. The building was quiet with no indication of a repeat performance of yesterday. The building tension had dissipated and semi-normality had returned.

My seven o'clock appointment was on time. He was short, rotund, and balding on the crown of his head. The extra weight he carried hung around his middle and looked like a truck inner tube. He was one of those individuals that no matter how expensive his clothes, he still looked sloppy and wrinkled, even with a coat and tie.

Rather than asking my secretary to send him into my office, I went to the outer office and introduced myself. "Hello, I am Mack Hargis. I think we have an appointment this morning? Mr. Russel, is that correct?"

"No, that is not correct! It is Dr. Russel. I am a professor at Aquinas College," he bluntly replied.

"I apologize, Dr. Russel. Would you please come into my office?"

He was obviously very proud of his degree and university position?

As we entered the office, I asked him to have a seat, and he chose the chair directly across the center of my desk. The chair was old and somewhat lower than the others. The springs were weak, causing a soft cushion. He sat down, and his weight caused him to sink deeply into the chair's cushion, which forced him to have to look up to me.

I said, "Mr. Ru...huh.... Dr. Russel, I think you wanted to discuss the dress code. Is that correct?"

"Yes, it is!" he replied in a huffy voice. "How can you possibly think you have the right to tell these students how to dress at this public school?"

I listened as he waved his arms and shoulders while bobbing up and down on the soft cushion springs. The view from my position would have been funny, except for his attitude. He reminded me of a young Boston bulldog pup trying to climb out of his deep-seated sleeping box. I listened for several minutes as he quoted laws and civil rights decisions. He was intelligent and well researched. After listening to his well-planned defense of freedom for the students, I asked, "Dr. Russel, you are a professor at Aquinas College, correct?"

"Yes, that is correct."

"Does the college have guidelines for employee dress?"

"Yes, they have general dress requirements" was the quick reply.

Well, I said, "If Aquinas College has a dress code, then how is Hillwood different?"

He snapped back, "Aquinas is a private institution, and therefore, they can enforce any rule they deem necessary. Hillwood is a public institution and is paid for by the public. All rules and regulations should be approved by the students, teachers, and parents."

My first thought, which I did not release, from my mouth was *Bull crap*!

"Dr. Russel, by state law, I am responsible for everything that occurs at Hillwood High School, from the advanced placement studies to the poems on the restroom wall. I am also responsible for maintaining an environment that is conducive to learning and free of disruptions. Any action that I deem as a disruption to this environment will be eliminated."

He started to climb out of his low-riding chair and, with a red face, said, "You are abusing your power over these poor kids."

By this time, I was standing, watching him fight his way out of the chair. I almost offered my hand to help him but thought better.

"Dr. Russel, I am sorry you feel that way. I am doing what I think is best for the students, school, and community. My decision will stand."

My last statement was not well received. As we left my office, he turned and said, "You will hear from my attorney."

I followed him to the front door and said, "Dr. Russel, tell your son to come see me tomorrow, and we will get him back in his classes."

Dr. Russel turned and faced me with a smirk, "My son is in class now, wearing jeans that you would approve."

He threw open the door and left. I never saw him again.

As the days turned into a week, the small rebellion at Hillwood slowly drifted from the minds of the students. As graduation was around the corner, apparently, the students had bigger fish to fry, but not so the Hillwood community.

There were several letters to the editor that supported the decision to ban the wearing of holey jeans in high schools. Some letters chastised the Nashville newspaper for considering the subject news worthy. A few students had letters published in the community paper. One of these letters basically asked the community not to judge the Hillwood student body by those individuals on the front page of the Sunday paper.

I read the paper closely for articles written by Amy Gutman, the reporter who felt it was her duty to come to the rescue of students and their holey jeans. I thought she may be interested in doing a follow-up story on the jean's controversy. To my knowledge, she never visited Hillwood again. Interestingly, Ms. Gutman left her position with the *Nashville Tennessean* newspaper shortly after her article.

The protesting students were intelligent individuals, but I wondered who gave them the guidance to use strategy lifted straight from the 1970s protest playbook. All they needed to make the 1970s come alive was a VW bus with flowers painted on the side.

A few weeks before school was out for the summer, a committee was formed to draw up guidelines for a new Hillwood dress code. The committee was made up of teachers, student leaders, parents, an assistant principal, and two students from the rogue group. The next year, there would be no doubt about the Hillwood High School dress code.

Forced Enrollment of a Killer

It was one of those days almost through winter and knocking on the springtime door. Cold gray-looking clouds were hanging low-threatening rain, or would it be snow? Warm weather always increased the active nature of the young natives at schools throughout the city. I was looking forward to summer vacation, as were the students at Hillwood, and it was only twelve weeks away.

Gazing out my window, I was watching two crows that visited the campus about this time each day, looking for morsels of food the students dropped on the patio during lunch. They came on such a regular basis that I had named them Heckle and Jeckle. Today's menu was golden brown french fries and bits of a hot dog. I am sure the crows felt they had found the mother lode. The phone rang and interrupted my crow-watching serenity.

I answered, "Hillwood High School, Mack Hargis speaking."

The call was from my boss, John. His voice stern and serious as he said, "Mack, we have a slight problem, and I want you to handle it."

When the boss calls with a request, the answer is always, "Sure, John, I will do what I can."

He said, "You may or may not know there was a shooting in the Pearl school community. It took place after school hours, and a Pearl student was killed. The student who killed the other kid had his arraignment last Friday. The judge ordered him to remain in school until his trial."

I interrupted my boss and said, "That happened several weeks ago. I saw it in the paper. I thought the kid was in jail."

John continued, "The murder did happen three weeks ago. He was in jail until his hearing last Friday. The judge ordered the student released from jail and to remain in school until his trial."

"I don't think that is wise. What has that to do with me?"

"The murdered victim has a brother attending Pearl High School. We don't think it would be a good idea to put the shooter back there. This could cause undue problems and possibly another shooting if his brother tried to retaliate.

"Okay, I understand that, but what does that have to with me?"

"We are going to enroll the him in Hillwood. It's the closest school to his home."

I noticed his comment was not "We want to enroll" or "Will you enroll?" or "Do you have any thoughts on how to solve this situation?" It was "We are going to!"

"John, I don't know about—"

He interrupted and said sternly, "I am not asking, this is a court order, and we have no choice."

"Why Hillwood?" I asked, still looking for a way out.

John's short reply, "Closest school with transportation."

"John, this community won't stand for—"

John interrupted again, "It is a court order. There is no choice but to do it."

I hesitated and then replied, "I am going to drag my feet on this enrollment. I want you to understand that! Hillwood students don't need to be subjected to danger either."

Our conversation was abruptly terminated.

I glared out the window at Heckle and Jeckle gorging themselves on leftovers. It must be nice to have a free meal and then fly away far above earthly problems.

My first thought was to make a few well-placed phone calls to community leaders and sat back and watch all hell break loose. I really wanted to do it. This was another example of the judicial system making decisions concerning something they know nothing about. The distance between Hillwood and Pearl High School is eight miles. Mileage would not be a deterrent to someone who had his mind set on revenge. The judge's decision put Hillwood students in danger.

I did not tell anyone on the Hillwood staff about this problem because the rumor mill would work overtime and produce some wild stories that would only make things worse. I sat for several minutes, pondering the situation and trying to find a solution.

The same thought kept reoccurring, *Damn judge! He has to be crazy!*

All evening and half the next day, I spent every spare minute searching for an answer. Dragging my feet seemed to be my only solution. Even Heckle and Jeckle had not offered any advice as I watched them enjoy an early lunch. Then suddenly, the ringing of the phone destroyed my thoughts.

I answered the phone. "Hillwood High School."

"Hey, Mack" came from the phone. "This is Carl. I think John told you I was going to call."

"Yeah, he said one of you fellows was going to call and put a problem here at Hillwood."

"Yeah, but it is not us. It is the judge," he shot back defensively.

I said, "If the community finds out, there will be hell to pay."

"We thought of that and think the case will be tried shortly" was the reply.

"How shortly?" I demanded.

"Well, we don't know. It is up to the judge," he barked back. "I need to get you this information. My time is limited. I have someone waiting for me,"

I was given the bare information concerning the young man: phone number, address, and his grandmother's name. I faintly heard in the background, "Come on, Carl. The restaurant will be crowded."

Carl's parting comment was "Get right on this. The judge wants him in school."

Hanging up the phone, I said to myself, *Yeah, get right on it. I told John I was going to slow-walk it, and that is what I intend to do.*

I am sure Carl's pressing engagement was his buddies waiting for him to go to lunch. I turned to watch Heckle and Jeckle sail around the patio. I was beginning to envy those two birds.

Staying true to my word, I slow-walked the process. About four days later, I called Ms. Roberts, the grandmother. No one answered the phone.

I left the following message. "Ms. Roberts, this is Mack Hargis, principal of Hillwood High School. I would like to talk to you about Jerome's school attendance. Thank you."

I documented my call and was hoping that Jerome did not want to be in school. That would free me of enrollment responsibility and the Hillwood students of possible danger. It was four thirty, and my drive home was just in time for the rush hour traffic. At least my day was consistent.

The next day, my Jerome-doesn't-want-to-go-to-school theory was shot to Hades with one phone call. Ms. Roberts returned my call. We set up a meeting for next week. School would be out in seven weeks. I was still hoping to wait this thing out.

The days were dragging by, and a satisfactory solution was still eluding me.

This problem was weighing on my mind to the point that I had begun to lose interest in Heckle and Jeckle. I knew there would be a point when the central office pressure would come to bear. Little did I know how soon.

While in the middle of my conference with Heckle and Jeckle, the darn phone rang.

Answering, I heard, "Hey, Mack, this is Carl. How is it going with the Pearl student?"

"Carl, I have not started the enrollment. I told John that I was going to slow-walk it. That kid doesn't need to be here at Hillwood, you know that!"

Carl snapped back, "That is not the point, the judge sa—"

I cut him off by saying, "The judge is crazy. This is insane."

"Yeah," Carl said, "but he is still the judge"

"You better get on this" was Carl's parting words.

I am sure Carl went straight to John's office and said, "Hargis has not enrolled that kid at Hillwood yet."

The following morning, I got a phone call from John, and he was not happy with me. His voice was stern as he said, "Mack, you got that Pearl kid enrolled yet?"

My immediate reply was "I told you I was going to slow-walk this situation. You know this community will—"

John interrupted, "Get that kid in school tomorrow. You hear me!"

"I hear you," I said and hung up the phone.

Once again, I thought about making a couple of community calls and turning the dogs loose on the judge and the central office. Many of the people in the Hillwood community could pick up the phone and call the mayor, the governor, and, a few, the president of the United States. I really wanted to make those calls, but surely, there is another solution. To comply with my boss's request or, maybe a better word, would be order, I called Ms. Roberts and asked if she and Jerome could come to school at an earlier date.

"Mr. Hargis, we can come in this afternoon or the first thing in the morning."

"Ms. Roberts, tomorrow morning will be fine…uh, say about nine thirty?"

She replied, "We will be there."

My slow-walking days were over, and the problem could no longer be avoided. I had bought the Hillwood students and me about two weeks. Tomorrow was enrollment day.

The next morning at nine thirty, my secretary informed me that a mother was here to see me about enrolling her son. I came out of my office to greet them. What I saw was not what I was expecting; I was not sure what I expected, but this was not it.

Ms. Roberts was about five feet, four inches tall, slender, and did not have the typical grandmother appearance. She was neatly dressed in a cotton print dress that showed some wear. She appeared to be about fifty years old. My best description would be a pleasant-looking lady with an understandably concerned look on her face.

Jerome, on the other hand, was a complete surprise, neatly dressed in jeans and a sport shirt. He was slender, about five feet, ten inches tall, sitting straight in his chair with no back slouching. There was no indication he was a bad ass. If someone taught him how to act and dress, they had done an excellent job.

"Ms. Roberts, I am Mack Hargis, the principal."

Ms. Roberts stood and said, "Thank you so much for seeing us."

Jerome stood up, stuck out his hand, and said, "I am Jerome. It's a pleasure to meet you."

No one in the office paid any attention to the new student and his grandmother, as the cat had been kept in the bag. Even with the good impressions, I was still leery of having a murderer at Hillwood.

"Come into my office, and we will discuss your situation," I said.

As I closed the door, I said, "I am aware of why you are here and the circumstances that brought you here. I am not interested in going into those details as I am sure you don't want to rehash them. We are here to get Jerome in school."

Ms. Roberts answered in almost a whisper, "Thank you."

Jerome said nothing.

I directed my questions to Jerome. 'What grade are you in?

"At the end of this year, I will have enough credits to be a junior."

I looked at his record to see if we could match the courses he was taking at Pearl. It took until lunch period to complete his schedule. We had everything in order, and I was talking to Ms. Roberts about school rules and what bus Jerome would take to school when I noticed Jerome had a fixed stare out the window.

Jerome was looking at my buddies Heckle and Jeckle. They were sitting opposite one another with a long french fry between them. Heckle had one end of the fry and Jeckle the other end. There was no fuss or fight. They just gently ate the fry until they came beak to beak.

Jerome said, "Did you see that? They shared a french fry. Are they here all the time?"

I replied, "Yes, most of the time."

Jerome shook his head as he and Ms. Roberts got up to leave.

Making a final check of the enrollment information, I noticed there was no birth date on his schedule card.

"Wait a minute, you didn't put your birth date on the enrollment card. How old are you, Jerome?"

Jerome said, "I will be eighteen next month."

Then the answer hit me. "Jerome, you are a little behind in school, right?"

His head dropped, and he said, "Yes, sir, about a year."

With enthusiasm in my voice, I asked, "How would you like to get your diploma by the end of this year? I am talking about December."

Ms. Roberts answered for him, "Yes, Yes, Yes."

We sat back down, and I explained the Graduate Equivalency Diploma (GED) program and asked if they were interested. Both wanted to know how to get into the program.

The next morning, they came to Hillwood and followed my truck to the Nashville Tech School on White Bridge Road. We went into a counselor's office.

"I am the principal of Hillwood High School, and this is Jerome and his grandmother, Ms. Roberts. Jerome is almost eighteen and is interested in the GED program."

That is all I had to say. The counselor took over.

As I drove my truck back to school, I wondered, *How did all this come to such a smooth ending?* Must have been some divine guiding force or maybe even positive energy from Heckle and Jeckle. Who knows?

I did not report back to Carl or John. I would let them call me. I was afraid that quirky judge might not accept the GED program as a school.

THE LEARNING CURVE

My chosen profession, education, was not one that would provide the extras that one would like for his family, such as food, clothing, and shelter. No, seriously, an educator's salary would provide for the basic things, but the luxury items were always out of reach. Most educators carried an extra job.

My uncle, when he discovered my professional direction, came by to talk with me. He suggested an accounting career and coach part-time. A part-time accountant and a full-time educator/coach crossed my mind. If I were really good at accounting, maybe I could embezzle enough money to stay in education. Occasionally, my mind moves in strange ways. My uncle pressured me into taking an accounting a course. After the first month, I determined that accounting was not for me. I could handle single entry, but double entry did not make sense. Why enter it twice when once would keep up with the money? My embezzling days were never to be.

Teaching and coaching were enjoyable, but more income was needed to support my family to my expectations. With the encouragement of another teacher, real estate was the choice to increase income. We became partners and purchased an apartment house.

Shortly after purchasing the apartments, an economic decline hit the United States. Rents plummeted; individuals had difficulty paying three hundred dollars a month for a two-bedroom apartment. Our mortgage note stayed the same while rental income decreased. What to do? There was a government program commonly called Section 8 that would pay or supplement rent for low-income persons. We generally avoided this program due to the ridiculous rules and regulations that were required.

We had no choice. Either work with Section 8 personnel or go bankrupt. This program involved a society subculture, which was beyond my experience. As the apartments were rented, I became acquainted with the tenants, most of whom were on welfare and needed help climbing out of their dependent world. This became my new project and also the beginning of my learning curve.

There was a young mother, Lynn, with two children. Everyone called her Lynnie. She was a vivacious lady, full of fun, with a beautiful ear-to-ear smile. One sultry July day, Lynnie was sitting on the patio watching me repair her air-conditioner. After replacing wires and a circuit board, we were waiting for the time delay switch to allow the air-conditioner to start. Lynnie offered me a glass of sweet tea while we waited. During our conversation, I asked her if she would have any interest in getting a General Equivalency Diploma (GED) and maybe train for a job.

"I will take a look at the information if you bring it by and explain it to me."

I said, "Okay, I will be by in a few days."

The social work agencies were eager to furnish proper material, which included the procedure for enrolling in a training program. The first program consisted of learning how to conduct yourself in the work environment. Silly, I thought, everyone knows how to conduct him or herself in a work environment. Just a waste of time and money. That was not true!

Lynnie had never had a job. She had become pregnant at fourteen. Because she was too young to work and had a child. she began receiving money from social assistant programs that provided her with food stamps, utility allowance, and housing. With a child and no skills, a job was beyond her reach.

Lynnie did well in the work environment training due to her pleasing personality and was enrolled in a keypunch class. After a short time, I received a call from the social worker assigned to Lynnie; she had not been in class for a week. The other class members thought she had quit. The social worker was hoping I might encourage her to come back.

In situations such as these, as strange as it seems, the first thing you think about is yourself. *How dare Lynnie quit the class! I have too much time, energy, concern, and even money tied up in that woman for her to quit. I had told everyone she would do well. Now she quits!*

Still angry, I went directly to her apartment, but she would not open the door.

I yelled, "I know you are home. I have a key. I'm coming in. You better open the door."

I really did not have the key, but the bluff worked, and Lynnie opened the door. Her head was lowered, and her eyes were red from crying. I went into the house, and we sat on her worn couch. Her big tears calmed me down.

In a calmer, more subdued voice, I asked, "What in the devil made you quit school? This is your chance to get out of here."

Lynnie looked at me with alligator tears streaming down her cheeks. This image is burned into my mind like a brand on a steer.

She said through sobs, "Mr. Mack, what if I don't pass?"

This answer nearly knocked me off the sofa. I thought, *Not pass, even if you don't pass, you will not be any worse off than you are now.* In my mind, not passing was not the sin. Not trying was the big sin. That was not her issue. My learning curve was making a sharp turn that I had not anticipated.

"If I don't pass, they will make fun of me."

"Who in the world would make fun of you?"

As she explained, I began to understand. There is a pecking order within the, for lack of a better word, welfare community. Word had leaked out that Lynnie was trying to improve herself. In the eyes of her community, she was trying to become better than they were.

Therefore, she was the focal point of her neighbors. She did not want to bear the brunt of ridicule from her neighbors and friends. If she failed, the jokes would turn from bugging to outright laughter and degrading remarks about her intelligence.

Many times, we make the mistake thinking the lower socio-economic class has no pride, sits around all day watching television, eating candy, and have no concern about improving their situation. Those individuals that are thrust into this environment (through no fault or error of their own) take the situation for what it is and try to make the best of it. We "do-gooders" with the best of intentions really don't understand.

REFLECTIONS

What was the success-failure ratio of the court-ordered integration experiment in the Nashville public school system? The true answer may not come clear for a hundred years or more. Historians will determine the value of the program and its extension of equal opportunities.

Equal opportunity and basic rights are not a question of socio-economic or racial status but God-given rights. No one should be prevented access to these rights for any reason. As Viktor Frankl states in *Man's Search for Meaning*, "Nobody has the right to treat another person poorly even if you've been treated poorly yourself." Even when these rights are available, how one takes advantage of these opportunities is a different matter.

The method in which these rights were extended to African Americans in Nashville, Tennessee, was not as successful as it might have been. The creator of the program, Dr. James Coleman, later stated that his busing theory failed even though the highest court in the nation approved busing as a means of desegregation. These laws were passed by individuals who would not participate in implementing them or be personally affected by the results.

One unintended consequence of rapid desegregation was decreased community support. When students attended local schools, distance was not a factor in supporting student activities. The school was the center of the community.

Much of the black school social structure was completely destroyed. This was not an intentional effort of school officials. In fact, great efforts were made to continue many of these events, but when the student population is suddenly decreased from 100 percent to 10 or 15 percent, it is difficult for any group to maintain its culture.

The black students carried the brunt of being bused out of their community. The distance from their home to the new school would many times be in excess of ten miles. Without after-school transportation, many black students were virtually eliminated from extracurricular activities.

"White flight" is a term given to the action of white families moving out of the county to avoid busing. The parents that could afford this flight were generally from the higher socioeconomic group that had supported their child's school financially and with parental leadership.

Along with white flight, there was an explosion of private schools, most of which found their basis and support from local churches. These budding private schools met in churches until funds could be procured for building construction. These two elements reduced the student population in the Nashville school system by twenty thousand.

The first few years of integration, the school board was understandably primarily invested in complying with the impossible court order of maintaining a ratio of 20 percent black students in each school. Educating students was put on the back burner. Maintaining a safe environment was the primary concern. Teachers did their best, but classroom management became foremost in their minds.

Could integration of the schools have been accomplished in a smoother and more civil matter? In my opinion, yes. The process would have taken longer, but this was not acceptable to the plaintiff. They pushed the legal system for more rapid and expanded change as they appealed the lower court's decision. They were understandably tired of city officials' slow response to the original court order of May 17, 1954. The appealed court decision resulted in additional chaos as it disrupted more communities by increasing the amount of busing. A slower and more humane community-based approach might have given students a better opportunity to understand and bond with one another.

A case in point came to the surface many years after my retirement. I was renovating a house and needed help because the job had escalated beyond my ability to complete the work on time. Nashville's economy was booming, and finding good help was very difficult. While picking up a few groceries at Kroger's, I saw a former student, Bill Benz and his wife, Johana.

As we talked, I asked, "What are you doing now?"

His reply was a godsend for me as he said, "I work in construction, renovating and repairing houses."

"I could use your help if you are not booked."

"I am busy, but I can work you into the schedule."

The working me into the schedule was sooner than I anticipated. The next week, we started working and talking about old times. He related the following event to me that exemplifies what could have happened with community-based integration.

Bill entered the seventh grade during the first phase of the Nashville integration program that allowed students to attend the closest school. Bill, being a good athlete, participated in all sports, along with the newly enrolled black students. His parents were very supportive of the school and, on many occasions, supplied transportation to and from the games. Bill became friends with Andrew Starling, a black teammate. One afternoon after practice, Bill and Andrew were in the dressing room talking.

Bill said, "Hey, Andrew, you want to come home with me and eat dinner."

Andrew, looking somewhat surprised and pleased, said, "Huh, huh, sure, I would like that."

Bill and Andrew entered the house unannounced. At first, Bill's family was a little taken aback seeing Bill's visitor. They quickly adjusted and had a pleasant meal.

Years later at a class reunion, Bill was talking with Andrew and said, "Do you remember when I asked you to come to my house and have dinner?"

Andrew replied, "Yeah, Bill, I sure do."

"What did you think when I asked you?"

Andrew smiled and, after thinking for a moment, said, "Bill, that was a milestone."

Bill also told me that Andrew was one of the first people to call him when he was going through heart surgery.

Bill and Andrew went their separate ways after graduation, but there is a mutual respect and bond that will last a lifetime. Both, if in need, feel free and with confidence to call on the other. This is what could have been accomplished through the integration process if time and common sense had prevailed. Opening quality education to all and developing a mutual respect should have been the goal, not percentages.

Has the integration process had positive benefits? Yes, black and white individuals have come to know and better understand one another thus lessening blanket racial prejudice. It also appears the majority of the public is developing an increased prejudice toward unlawful, violent actions, no matter the race. But listening to the media and some politicians, one would assume the opposite. While serving on the Nashville school board and attending a conference on violence in schools, this attitude was brought to light. During a discussion, my friend and successful African American basketball coach Cornelius Ridley stated during a group discussion, "I don't care what color he is. If he tries to take what I have worked hard for, he is going to meet strong resistance."

A large portion of at-risk students are not taking advantage of educational opportunities that are available to them. Students need more support and pressure from their community. I have heard very few leaders publicly chastise students for lack of academic success. It is easier to say failure was caused by something else, such as poor teachers, not enough money, or poor learning ability. I firmly believe any student entering school ready and eager to learn with teacher encouragement will be successful.

A friend, who was director of a small school system, approached his board of education, asking them to fund a project for mostly black at-risk students. Shortly after the meeting, a board member privately said to him, "Why do you want to spend money on that group? Don't you know some people just can't learn?"

The sad part of this statement is that national dropout rates and test scores are proving him right! Can he be proven wrong? Can this trend be corrected?

Yes, there are ways to encourage students and parents to value education. These plans only need to be organized and implemented. *It takes a village to raise a child* is an African proverb that can be slightly changed to meet our national situation. *It takes a nation working together to change our youth's direction.*

Laws eliminating discrimination do not solve the problem. In reality, they may cause the problem to increase or go underground. Going underground is much like an infection that appears to be healed on the surface but is festering and builds until it erupts, sometimes causing permanent and irreparable damage. Decisions such as busing, forcing both black and white communities to disrupt their lives in one day, is a prime example. If social change is to remain positive and permanent, change must move slowly with understanding and creating brotherly respect.

The comment that even Mother Nature reacts violently to sudden change can be compared to the actions of individuals during court-ordered busing. Much as hurricanes, tornadoes, and earthquakes cause massive damage that takes years to repair, so is it with humans and social repair. This social repair cannot be accomplished by laws and courts alone. It must also be carried out on an individual basis.

This psychological approach is one of individual contact. As we move through our daily activities, we come in contact with many diverse individuals. Effort should be made to have a social interaction with these individuals if no more than a "hello" or "good morning." My short experience with this social interaction theory has met with some interesting results.

Recently, my wife and I were having lunch at O'Charley's. We were facing a table of five women, four black and one white. Each time I glanced up, I found myself staring into the face of an attractive black lady at that table. As people normally do, we each quickly looked in another direction as if to say, "I wasn't looking at you."

After ordering our meal, my wife, a retired teacher, said, "Those ladies are acting like teachers on their lunch break from in-service."

"Yes, they do. You remember how enjoyable it was to go lunch at a restaurant like normal people?"

We both laughed at past memories of our educational backgrounds as I continued to play peep pie with the lady at the other table.

"I would bet my paycheck they are a bunch of teachers."

My wife replied rather forcibly, "Why don't you go over there and ask them? You have talked about them our entire meal. Go on. They are about to leave."

"Okay, by darn, I will."

Moving to their table, I engaged my peep pie partner and said, "Excuse me, I am a retried high school principal, and I was wondering if y'all are teachers?

"No, we are not teachers," replied the lady.

"Well, you sure act like teachers on their lunch break from in-service."

She smiled and said, "I am so glad you came over. I thought you were looking at us because there were four black women with one white."

I laughed and said, "Why should that make a difference?"

As she walked away, she said, "You know how some people are?"

We finished our meal and drove to Sears for my wife to return an item. I waited in the car. She came out of Sears smiling.

"What are you smiling about? You look like you just won the lottery."

"You know that lady you talked with at O'Charley's?"

"Yeah"

"She saw me from a couple of isles over and sent me a big smiley wave and said hi."

Don't know who she is and probably will never see her again, but we connected.

Another case in point was during halftime at a Vanderbilt football game. I went to the restroom that was crowded as usual. Making my way out was an ordeal. Fans were so thick in the main corridor that a short person could become asphyxiated. I forced my way to the section R stadium entrance to get out of the main flow of concession-stand-starved spectators. As I escaped the crowd, I noticed another individual had done the same thing.

Leaning against the wall, I turned to the gentleman next to me, a tall well-dressed middle-aged black man, and said, "I wonder how much urine flows through these pipes at halftime."

He smiled and said, "I was thinking the same thing. How much water is used at halftime?"

We both smiled, and then he said, "At least they have upgraded to individual urinals. I did not like the old trough style where everybody was pushed together with no privacy."

"Yeah, you never knew who was looking at what."

"Exactly."

"A friend of mine was in Atlanta last year. He went to the restroom, and while using the facility, another individual stepped to the adjacent urinal. The man leaned over toward my friend and said, 'Nice one.'"

We were laughing when his wife came, grabbed his arm, and said, "We are going to miss the kickoff. Let's go."

They headed up the entrance ramp, and after about four or five steps, he stopped, turned, and waved. In a loud clear voice rising above crowd noise, he said, "Nice One," laughing and smiling as he moved away.

One major point that I sincerely believe is, "WE WILL NEVER GET ALONG WITH ONE ANOTHER UNTIL WE LEARN TO LAUGH AT ONE ANOTHER WITH ONE ANOTHER."

A few months ago, I went by my daughter's rental unit. Vince, the person renting, was sitting on the front porch with his friend Robert.

Vince handed me the rent and said, "I am having trouble with the neighbor again. I don't know what to do. I keep this place in good shape and the yard mowed and trimmed."

"What are they complaining about?" I replied.

"Oh, they say I have too many cars. I have four cars, and they all run and are parked in the driveway."

Robert chimed in, "Maybe the cars are not expensive enough."

I said, "Maybe."

After looking at Vince for a few seconds, I said, "You know what the real problem is?"

"No, what is it?"

"Yeah, you do, Vince. You are black."

Vince quickly replied, "You are probably right, but there is nothing I can do about that."

I said just as rapidly, "I don't know. I have a gallon of bleach in the back of the truck. A bleach bath might solve the problem."

Before either Vince nor I could open our mouth, Robert said, "That won't work for Vince. He would come out looking like a Zebra."

All three of us laughed until our sides hurt. We sat quietly for a few minutes, regaining our composure and breath.

"Robert, man you should be a stand-up comic. You are funny," I replied.

"I have been told that before."

We parted company with smiles on our faces while realizing that we still had a closed-minded individual in the house next door.

On another occasion, I was in Office Depot to buy some over-priced printers ink. After finally forcing myself to choose the seventy-nine-dollar tiny package of ink, I moved to the checkout lane. As I was approaching the line, another customer stepped in front of me. It was not as if he had hurried to cut me off; he was just a millisecond ahead of me. Standing behind him, I began to closely analyze him. He was large enough to be a professional football player. The longer I looked at him, the more amazed I became. I began to understand why those one-hundred-ninety-five-pound running backs are so fast. They are running for their lives.

During my thoughts, he had to step back to let another customer through the line. I did not react fast enough, and he knocked the ink cartage from my hand. Before I could recover, he snatched it from the floor. Looking down at me with a stern look on his face, he pushed the ink cartage toward me and said in a deep voice, "Sorry."

I took the item while looking up at him. My neck felt much like it did when I first saw the Empire State Building. I will surely develop a crick in my neck from hyperextension.

I said, "Thank you."

Then suddenly, my thoughts when straight to my tongue by passing my brain and shot out of my mouth when I said bluntly, "How did you get so big?"

We were second in line to checkout, and several people were standing in earshot of our one-sided conversation.

The enormously large man stared down at me and said in a gruff voice, "By eating my vegetables."

Everyone was silently waiting to hear my reply and to see if he was going to break ever bone in my body. Then a big smile came across his face as he continued, "You didn't eat yours, did you?"

Friendly Giant

Those comments caused an outbreak of laughter. The cashier was laughing so hard that all transactions halted. She was holding onto the counter to keep from falling to the floor.

I laughingly replied, "I wish I had."

After everyone regained their composure, I gave the cashier my phone and asked her to take our picture. I showed him the picture, and he repeated, "Vegetables man, eat your vegetables."

We laughed again and went our separate ways.

The focus of this one-man social experiment is that we should stop trying to surmise what the other person is thinking; we need to talk with him. Reach out to individuals with a smile, a joke, or just a pleasant nod. They will respond in kind.

To advance this social experiment, ignoring what many elected officials, mainstream media, and some clergy spew out over the social and mainstream media is imperative. Just interact with the person next to you with a smile. His response will be pleasant, and you will have made a small step toward social peace.

ABOUT THE AUTHOR

Dr. J. Mack Hargis spent twenty-five years as a teacher, coach, and principal within the Metro Nashville Public Schools (MNPS), earning his PhD from Vanderbilt University's Peabody College. After retiring, he served on the MNPS school board, taught at several regional universities, including Tennessee State University, Trevecca University, Indiana Wesleyan University, and Cumberland University, as well as working as an educational consultant across Tennessee. His staff development seminars have been presented for school systems throughout Tennessee, and Alabama including specialty schools such as the Tennessee School for the Blind.

In addition to the MNPS school board, Dr. Hargis served on the Nashville High School Principal Association (president), the Committee on Violence Prevention for MNPS (chairman), MNPS's Technology Committee (co-chair), and as the Nashville Retired Teachers Association's legislative chairman. He was honored by the Tennessee Athletic Directors Association as the Athletic Director of the Year, MNPS's Administrator of the Year, and was included in Who's Who in American Education.

Other publications by Dr. Hargis include articles in the National Education Secretary, Tennessee Teacher, and Media and Methods, as well as co-authoring two books, *School Consolidation: Points to Ponder* and *Retirement and Financial Planning for Educators*.

Beyond his professional service, Dr. Hargis has also served his community as a member of the Madison Chamber of Commerce Executive Board and the Nashville Parks and Recreation board. He has two daughters, Heather Hargis and Rachel Kennedy; son-in-law, Steve Kennedy; and grandchildren, Connor and Lauren. He currently resides in Madison, Tennessee, with his wife, Ann, and dog, Toby.

CPSIA information can be obtained
at www.ICGtesting.com
Printed in the USA
JSHW050743010621
15333JS00001B/26

9 781646 544875